The COMPLETE FIGHT For Your MARRIAGE BOOK

By Lambert and Kim Sands

A Production of
Marriage Mechanics Ministries, Intl

Copyright 2014 © by Marriage Mechanics Ministries, Intl. Inc.
All rights reserved

No part or portion of this book can be used or reproduced by any means: graphic, electronic or mechanical, including photocopying, audio recording, or any information system storage system without the expressed written permission of the author or Marriage Mechanics, Ministries, Inc. except in the case of brief quotations embodied in critical articles and reviews.

All scriptures taken from the King James Version of the Bible.

Copies of this book can be purchased directly from Marriage Mechanics Ministries, Inc. 2061 Watersedge Dr. Deltona, FL. 32738
(407) 385 8201

Lambert Sands is an ordained minister
and has produced this work under the inspiration of the Holy Spirit.

ISBN: 978-0-9911546-4-7 (paperback)
ISBN: 978-0-9911546-5-4 (Ebook)

Printed in the United States of America
Marriage Mechanics Ministries, Inc. 12/03/2014

*We dedicate this book to the many
husbands and wives who refuse to give up
even when things look gloomy and hopeless.
Your perseverance in the midst of hardship,
rejection, and sometimes loneliness,
has inspired this book
I stand in agreement with you that God
is still on the throne and nothing is impossible
with him. Stay strong in faith and remember ...
You don't have to wait until the battle is over,
You can shout the victory now!!*

Contents

Part One 11
Fight For Your Marriage 11
Introduction 13
1. Prepare to Fight 15
2. Know Your Enemy 21
3. Spirits in Operation 26
    Family Spirits 28
    Spirits That Enter Through Being Unequally Yoked .. 28
    Spirits of Strife 30
4. Weapons that Work 33
    Use The Word To Protect Your Marriage 35
    When You Lose a Skirmish 36
    Here are just a few scriptures to encourage and use against the enemy attacks. 36
        Assurance of Salvation 36
        Blessings 37
        Assurance of Victory 37
        In Need of Encouragement 38
        In Need of Protection 38
        Hopeless Situation 38
5. Making Reconciliation Work 39
    A Prayer for Deliverance and Protection 43
Part Two 45

Understanding Male Authority 45
Introduction 47
6. The Awakening 49
    Who Am I? 50
    Authority Lost 52
    The Hiding Place 53
7. Walking in Divine Authority 56
    Authority and the Wife 60
8. Passivity: The Leadership Killer 64
    Pathway to Dominion 66
    What is prosperity? 71
    God Plan For Financial Prosperity 73
    Freedom From Self the Way to Excellence 78
Part Three 81
Understanding Her Feminine Side 81
Introduction 83
9. I Love My Husband! 85
10. Welcome to Motherhood 92
11. Keeper of the Home 100
    Hints for the Homemaker 107
12. A Meek & Quiet Spirit 110
13. Highly Favored 115
Part Four 117
Understanding Why We Fuss & Fight 117
Introduction 119
14. Pressures & Problems 121

15. Having a Good Fight 125

16. Drop the Bags...Honey! 129

Handling Rejection 134

17. Exercising Control 135

Intellectual Control 136

Sexual Control 137

Monetary Control 139

Psychic Control 141

18. When the Devil Comes!! 144

19. Divine Unity 151

Part Five 153

Victory in the Bedroom 153

Introduction 155

20. The Problem 157

21. Her Side 159

22. His Side 161

23. The Truth 163

24. Deeper Problems 167

Sexual Addiction 167

Lack of Performance 169

25. Keeping Romantic Love Alive 171

Keep the Fire Burning 171

About Marriage Mechanics 173

Part One

Fight For Your Marriage

Introduction

When *Kim and I got married* on February 9, 1985, we were starry-eyed. Full of dreams and fantasies, we rushed to the Pocono Mountains, in Pennsylvania, to enjoy our much-anticipated honeymoon. However, before the end of the week, we had our first argument. Yes, right on the honeymoon! We enjoyed the remainder of our honeymoon but this was indeed a foretaste of things to come.

Over the years of our marriage, we enjoyed the bliss that marriage can bring. We have also experienced the downside of arguments and bickering. Like us, you may have also entered marriage with a one-sided view, not realizing that you are in the fight of your life. To save your marriage, you must fight!! Marriage has now become the battleground of the millennium.

Most people spend their time fighting each other, totally oblivious to their unseen enemy. Satan is our enemy, not our wives or husbands. He is the invisible foe sowing discord and feeding bitterness. He is the one that advises divorce. He is behind the adultery, uncontrollable anger, and abuse. *Ephesians 6:12 says, "For we wrestle not against flesh and blood, but against principalities, against powers, against the rulers of the darkness of this world against spiritual wickedness in high places."*

We must resist him! We must get off the ropes of despair and get back in the center of the ring, and fight!! The purpose of this book is to inspire those who have given up hope; renew trust in those who feel betrayed; and strategy to those who want to fight! Don't quit, lift up those tired hands! Put on your spiritual gloves! *"One man of you shall chase a thousand: for the Lord your God, he it is that fighteth for you, as he hath promised you." (Joshua 24:7).*

—LAMBERT & KIM

1. Prepare to Fight

M*ichael cringed in the corner of his bedroom* holding his stuffed Barney Bear. His little eyes, filled with tears darted uncontrollably from parent to parent. Whap! Bang! Crash! It was a full-scale battle. "Richard, I hate you......I hate you," cried Michael's mother as she threw a second figurine at his father who had just slapped her across the face. His father retreated to the living room where he began to hurl insults. "I wish I'd never married a lousy woman like you. You make me sick. I had enough of your stupidity and stubbornness. Tomorrow I'm going to the lawyer's office and file for a divorce." Slam! The front door was shut abruptly and the irate father marched briskly toward the family car. Shoving the key into the ignition, Richard quickly pulled off, his feet slamming the gasoline pedal to the floor. He was determined to follow through on his threats.

"I want my daddy, I want my daddy." Michael quickly jumped to his feet and ran toward the front door hoping to stop his father from leaving. But before he could reach the front door Paige grabbed him. "Your father is not coming back. We don't need him. He's a no good man." Michael struggled to get out of his mother's arms. He wanted his father. He wanted his mother and father back together. He wanted everyone to be happy, but his whole world was crumbling around him. Wiggling himself loose, Michael ran outside but the car had already disappeared into the night. "Daddy, Daddy, come back! Daddy, Daddy, Daddy.........."

It was a long night for Paige. It was nearly 2 A. M. before she could get Michael to sleep. Lying was the only way to appease his fears. Paige told him that daddy was only gone for a few days. But Paige knew that her husband was serious, and would follow through with the divorce threat. Over the last several months, their marriage was any thing but good. There were constant arguments and fights from money to who should be in charge. Paige wondered why she had gotten married any way. Marriage had only brought her misery. Yes, maybe divorce is the answer, she thought to herself as she popped several Tylenol tablets into

16 | The Complete Fight for Your Marriage Book

her mouth to relieve her migraine headache. As she drifted off to sleep, Paige thought about just her and Michael playing together at their favorite park in Winter Springs, just the two of them!

It was midnight when Richard reached the Days Inn Hotel. He had lost track of time. Anger had totally consumed him and he had unconsciously driven ninety miles on the interstate highway. He got a room and retired to the bed. The comfortable, warm bed did nothing for him, he was still angry. Making Paige pay for her stubbornness was all he thought about. Tomorrow, he would explain everything to his lawyers. Proving that she was an unfit mother would not be hard. She spent too much time at her office and was never at home to take care of Michael. Then there was the time she overdosed on sleeping pills. "Yea, I'll get custody of Michael," he thought to himself. Drifting off to sleep, he imagined the emotional turmoil that Paige would have when he got custody. He would win after all!

Every year, the odds of a marriage failing continues to rise as husbands and wives find themselves on different sides of the marital battlefield. As the above story illustrates, instead of fighting for the marriage and finding solutions, the tendency is to retreat in fear or to find the easy way out of a bad situation. The Apostle Paul said, "In the last days perilous times will come, for men shall be lovers of their own selves, covetous, boaster, proud, blasphemers, disobedient to parents, unthankful, unholy, without natural affection, trucebreakers, false accusers, incontinent, fierce, despisers of those that are good, traitors, heady, high-minded, lovers of pleasures more than lovers of God; having a form of godliness, but denying the power thereof....... " (2 Timothy 3:1-5). This scripture points toward a time of unthinkable arrogance, moral decay and selfishness in society. A time when all relationships whether business, personal or family would be in danger of collapse. **That time has come!**

No one is exempt from the fight. No one! From Hollywood to the middle class suburbs, to the impoverished of inner cities, divorce has become commonplace. Divorce, once a taboo word in earlier times among married people, has become the easy way out of a bad relationship. Even the church has not escaped the powerful talons of divorce.

Now, even among the sanctified, the evil forces of hell have inflicted serious damage. Religious leaders and lay members alike, have found their marriages under attack. The once unthinkable notion that a Pastor, or Minister of the Gospel should be divorced, is now becoming the norm. Churches are packed with divorced people as fewer and fewer Christians are willing to weather the storms of marriage life. What a mockery Satan is making of Christianity. If the Saints can't make it, who can?

You see, the enemy knows that marriage forms the foundation of family life, and this is the main reason he constantly attacks the sacredness of marriage. When God united Adam and Eve in holy matrimony, it was the beginning of the family. The relationship of a husband and wife is designed to be a guide and living portrait of love and unity. When a husband and wife truly love each other, their children learn relationship skills i.e. how to love, how to confront, selflessness, team work and the like. They are also reared with a sense of security. However, when the marriage relationship is destroyed, the family, community and nation all suffer.

However, we can fight back and win! First, we must recognize that we are in a fight. The moment you said, "I do", your relationship moved to another level. All hell is now aware that the commitment is now a divine covenant. Satan and his cohort, desiring to destroy anything that is of God, bring in reinforcements to attack the marriage. Many couples who have known each other for years, or have even lived together, often wonder why their trouble intensified after the wedding. Satan had nothing to lose before the covenant; in fact, he had more to gain if he could keep the couple in an unlawful and unholy relationship. Now, with a consummated marriage, **your marriage represents a threat to his kingdom.**

Next, we must recognize that this battle is spiritual and not physical. Save your words! Stop bickering! Shhhhh! We must get in the spiritual realm to fight a spiritual enemy. Our only recourse and counter attack is to expose his covert operations. We must become like the American soldier who wears night vision goggles that illuminate his vision even when it is pitch dark.

With this special night-wear, he can see in the darkness like it was broad daylight. This gives him the advantage over the enemy and shifts the balance of war in his favor. We too must put on our night goggles and master the night! It's pitch dark outside and we need the illumination of the Holy Spirit like never before to defeat our most elusive enemy.

Our next step is to be prepared. Like an old adage says, "If you fail to prepare, then, prepare to fail." Jesus taught a simple lesson in Luke 14:26-33 about discipleship, and how important it was to fully count the cost of discipleship. In other words, to be victorious disciples require more than mere zeal and excitement; qualities that most married couples usually have in abundance.

Jesus explained that if a king made a war against another king, he should first sit down and consult with the wise men in his kingdom. They would need to know whether they had sufficient resources to defeat the opposing forces, and if not, it would be better to send an ambassador to the opposing forces, conceding defeat. This is precisely what is happening in marriages today: no preparation, no consultation, and the sad result is hopelessness, fear, and frustration. Few marriages are able to survive the onslaught of the enemy.

With limited knowledge, and training, most married partners are sitting ducks for Satan. In fact, most of them are the product of broken relationships, and without healing and reconciliation, they carry within them the tools of hatred and unforgiveness that Satan can use for his malicious schemes. The word of God declares in the book of Hosea, *"My people are destroyed for lack of knowledge".*

Finally, in the heat of the battle, most run to the divorce court instead of the prayer closet. For most families, the altar is television, video games and the Internet. However, I want to encourage you to pray. Having proven it in my own marriage, I am a witness that prayer changes things.

Indeed, God is still working miracles; miracles for those who are willing to look up and not down; miracles for those who are willing to fight, and wait on him. *"When the enemy comes in like a flood, the spirit of the Lord shall lift up a standard against him."* (Isaiah 59:19). *"The name of the Lord is a strong tower, the righteous runneth into it, and is safe."* (Proverbs 18:10). The promise of deliverance is to those who are willing to look beyond their circumstances to an immutable God, and to Jesus who boldly asserts that he has *"all power in heaven and in earth."* There is still power in the name of Jesus, and those who choose to call on that name can expect deliverance.

It is necessary to mention that people, who deliberately disobey good judgment, parental advice, and the guidance of the Holy Spirit, will indeed reap the results of their misguided and sometimes rebellious marriage decisions. But even then, the Holy Spirit is ready to forgive and give them the grace to endure.

Nonetheless, all marriages whether consummated with God's help and guidance or not, will be tested. *"...Nevertheless, such shall have trouble in the flesh..."* (1 Corinthians 7:28) The key to success is how you handle problems that come your way. Trouble was never meant to cause us to give up in despair; God allows trouble that we may be exposed to victory through the wonderful power and wisdom of God. For some people, there is an unwillingness to live with their decisions and accept the consequences of their choices. However, if we simply give our burdens to the Lord in true humility and repentance, he can work them out. *"And we know that all things work together for good to them that love the Lord and who are called according to his purpose."* (Romans 8:28) The very thing that Satan has used to derail our lives will give God the opportunity to prove his wonderful power and amazing glory.

I want to encourage those who read this book that I am in this same fight. I need the encouragement and motivation contained in this booklet just as much as you. Nobody is exempt from the attacks of the enemy. *"Whom resist steadfast in the faith, knowing that the same afflictions are accomplished in your brethren that are in the world."* (1

Peter 5:9). In fact, by writing this book, I have become a bigger target! If Satan can get me to fall, wouldn't it curtail the impact of this message?

Over the years of our ministry, Kim and I have seen the most ferocious attacks of the enemy. Kim was attacked with cancer and I was attacked with everything else; pride, fear, insecurity, sickness, and the list goes on. But my brothers, my sisters, God is still sovereign and we are still *"more that conquerors"*. I am simply thankful, appreciative and humbled that Jesus Christ of Nazareth would allow me to encourage his body in this area of ministry.

I encourage you to hold on, regardless of the cost. Being a soldier in God's army means that, we will have battles to fight. We will suffer pain and injury. We will be rejected and despised, but the spoils will be worth it all! As you turn the pages of this book, keep focused. Trouble won't last forever and this too will pass. In time, things will change, *your test will become your testimony and your mess will become your message.*

2. Know Your Enemy

When problems arise in our marriages, the tendency is to lash out at each other. Few people recognize the true enemy. Your enemy is not your husband; it is not your wife: it is the Devil. He is the enemy of God and the enemy of our souls. The Apostle Peter reinforces this when he says, *"Be sober be vigilant; because your adversary the Devil as a roaring lion walketh about, seeking whom he may devour!"* (1 Peter 5:8) However, because of Satan's very illusive tactics and deceptive behavior, most people are unable to detect his movements or presence. His many names and faces includes: Father of Lies, (Matthew 8:44); Your Adversary (1 Peter 5:8); Dragon (Revelation 20:2); Belial (2 Corinthian 6:15); Lucifer (Isaiah 14:12); Prince of the Power of the Air (Ephesians 2:2); The God of This World (2 Corinthian 4:4), and Accuser of the brethren (Revelation 12:10).

To understand Satan and his tactics, we must trace his origin. The enemy of our souls was once an ally of God working diligently in God's cabinet as a musician, light-bearer, and covering cherub or protector. He was called Lucifer, an arch, or chief angel, with numerous angels under his authority. As the story is related in Isaiah 14:12-20 and Ezekiel 28:12-19, his position, appearance, and wisdom "went to his head"; he became proud and vainglorious leading to eventual rebellion against God. He was no longer contented to be just an Indian, he wanted to be chief. He wanted to be God.

Of course, his ill-fated sedition was quelled and Lucifer was abruptly "kicked" out of heaven with a promise from God that his final judgment will come in due time. Since then, Satan, as he is now called, continues to live in rebellion, and uses every opportunity to resist and attempt to frustrate the plans of the Almighty.

Satan is not omnipresent, omniscient or omnipotent but he is very clever, and he uses his organized entourage of fallen angels to make up for his lack of mobility. These demons, along with Satan are unceasingly active to side-track human beings from a godly pathway. *"In whom the god of this world hath blinded the minds of them which believe not, lest*

22 | The Complete Fight for Your Marriage Book

the light of the glorious gospel of Christ, who is the image of God, should shine unto them." (2 Corinthians 4:4)

As Satan's many names or aliases infer, his modus operandi centers on deception, lies, and impersonation. The mind is the doorway to the soul, and by using the mind as his doorway, Satan can springboard his attacks of lies and deception on the unsuspecting and ignorant. When an individual is unaware that his thoughts are originating from a foreign source, he is an easy victim of the Devil's devices and can be controlled and manipulated without even realizing it.

An un-renewed mind, pride, fear, insecurity, unforgiven sin (adultery, theft, lies etc), past abuse (incest, molestation, etc.) and the like, gives Satan leverage to launch assaults on a person's mind. Satan and his evil imps will get your mate to fall into sin: infidelity, abuse, insincerity etc. Then he turns to the other mate and say "see what they have done, look how many times he/she has done it, you don't have to live with this." **His aim is to create a spirit of bitterness and animosity in the marriage that will eventually lead to separation and divorce.**

Satan's greatest ploy, however, is impersonation or transformation. To pretend that he is not really present, and then masquerade in the clothing of a Christian. **Dressing up as a religious leader or fellow Christian layman, is his most effective means of doing damage in the church world.** *"For such are false apostles, deceitful workers, transforming themselves into the apostles of Christ. And no marvel; for Satan himself is transformed into an angel of light." (2 Corinthian 11:13-14)* In fact, this will be one of his final acts when he comes in the form of a messiah as the antichrist.

In this disguise, he can teach that divorce is the only way out of a bad marriage. He can also lure people into a marriage with someone whom they thought was a Christian, only to find out later that the person was a hypocrite, a fraud and a pretender. To defeat him on this front requires a sensitive and intimate relationship with the Holy Spirit and the gift of discerning of Spirit. Let me say this unequivocally: spiritual sensitivity is no longer an option in this new millennium, it's

mandatory. Jesus said, *"For there shall arise false Christ, and false prophets, and shall shew great signs and wonders; insomuch that, if it were possible, they shall deceive the very elect."* *(Matthew 24:24)* We live in perilous times, and our only recourse is to forge deep spiritual relationship with Jesus Christ.

Discerning of Spirits is a spiritual gift, (1 Corinthians 12:10). This means that it is given by the Holy Spirit to designated individuals as the need arises. He (The Holy Spirit) equips people to see into the spiritual realm. This allows the illuminated person to perceive whether by a vision or by the inner witness of the Holy Spirit, the presence of demons or the true attitudes of the human spirit.

Many times during our marriage counseling sessions, God would illuminate my wife and me to the true problems and attitudes, which were totally contrary to what the counselees were putting forth. **They were deceived into the playing the blame game instead of looking into their own hearts.** As long as Satan can hide, he can continue his success in a marriage relationship.

Additionally, any believer who has fine tuned his spiritual senses through prayer and study of God's word in addition to a committed relationship with the Lord can use his "spiritual senses" to discern his environment. *"For every one that useth milk is unskillful in the word of righteousness: for he is a babe. But strong meat belongeth to them that are of full age, even those who by reason of use have their senses exercised to discern both good and evil."* *(Hebrews 5:12-13)*

A good example of Satan's tactics on an individual is the story of Job. Job's fight with Satan and his final vindication in the end, give us a summary of Satan's work against the Christian and God's position when testing times come. Satan attacked Job's finances, then his children. When this did not ruffle Job's faith in God, Satan requested that God allow him further access to Job.

He then infected Job with a skin disease that brought tremendous suffering. But it still did not end there. The marriage came under attack. Job's wife in the heat of the battle decided that it was time to throw in the towel! It was time to give up! "Curse God and die," she told Job. But the man of God refused to accept defeat. In the midst of his anguish and pain, Job rebuked his wife for her remarks, and worshiped God!

But even then, the fate of this stalwart continued on a path of anguish, rejection and persecution when his friends, instead of bringing encouragement, heaped depression and accusations on him. They insisted that God was punishing him for his own wickedness and secret sins. (I want to inject here that it's very important that you get good advice when going through a marital problem. Avoid people who cast blame. Avoid people who point you to the divorce court. Rather look for someone who will give you sound advice and a word of faith.)

After Job had patiently endured, God himself answered Job and blessed him abundantly. This is what people who faithfully and patiently endure can expect: God will "show up" and bless them abundantly and beyond their wildest expectations. *"Now unto him that is able to do exceeding, abundantly above all that we ask or think, according to the power that dwelleth in us. Unto him be glory in the church by Christ Jesus throughout all ages world without end." (Ephesians 3:21-22)*

We must, however, keep in mind that God was always in control. God, in fact, instigated the battle by telling Satan about his outstanding servant, Job. This is a powerful statement that literally means that if I am upright with God, God must first sample all foods that are served on the plate of my life. Satan does not have the authority to serve anything on my table. And when he does, I know that God is ultimately in control and there is no need for alarm. If most people can only grasp this concept, we would have a lot more victorious Christians.

If we can recognize the enemy for who he really is, we can go through our trials with a praise on our lips and a song in our hearts. With our natural eyes we can only see a natural situation. It then becomes a problem that stresses us out. But with our spiritual eyes we can see God in control, allowing our enemy to test us to bring about a greater dimension of glory and power in our lives. At the end, Job was far richer and wiser. God himself had visited Job and talked with him.

The purpose of the trial was to bring Job to a deeper dimension of blessing and maturity. This is why David says in the Psalm 34, *"I will bless the Lord at all times his praise will continually be in my mouth."*

We need not subscribe to the voice of defeat. Your enemy wants you to give up. His aim is to get you turn your back on God. But the Devil is a liar and the truth is in him. Hang on; hold out; help is on the way. God has created you to live victoriously. He has written a contract out in His word for you, and has signed it with his own blood (through Jesus Christ). But if you never read or enter into the contract, you can never reap the benefits. The contract says in section Luke 10:19 *"Behold, I give unto you power to tread on serpents and scorpions, and over all the power of the enemy: and nothing shall by any means hurt you."*

3. Spirits in Operation

After a mad dash to the altar, many are disappointed when their fantasy for a "happily ever after" story does not materialize. Others arrive in marriage life satisfied that they have married Mr. or Mrs. Right, only to realize that their mates are riddled with faults and shortcomings. Their determination to correct these defects only leads to more heartache, disappointment, and depression. The truth is, everyone has faults and character problems that may take a lifetime for God to heal and correct. Bible characters like David, Solomon, Abraham, and Moses all showed that even the greatest of men can have character defects. But there are some character and behavioral problems that are the direct result of demonic activity; baggage that is secretly brought into the new marriage.

The difference between a character defect that needs healing and a problem that persists because of demonic activity can be summed up in one word: bondage. A person who has a vice that they are unable to conquer and are habitually and consistently susceptible to its power may need deliverance from demons. In other words, this is not a problem that can be overcome by psychological assistance or by implementing changes in one's daily routine. These are behavioral problems that persist, even after counseling and striving to change. Held captive by their vices, these individuals have no control and are repeat offenders of their crimes.

Many of these problems can be traced to previous experiences of abuse, sexual immorality, and corrupt associations. This is why premarital counseling is an absolute necessity during our time. A lot of people could be spared the anguish of a bitter marriage if proper premarital counseling techniques were employed; techniques that would have uncovered the bad generation past and ominous signs that can later destroy a marriage. These can include: a history of family members obtaining divorces, family history of sexual immorality and promiscuity, previous record of abuse, a family background of selfishness and excessive frugality; overly-introverted behavior;

witchcraft in the family, history of financial impropriety, and the like. However, most premarital counseling barely scrapes the surface, and usually leaves couples in a potentially doomed relationship.

A good example is a marital dilemma that I came in contact with. A young lady and her husband were having tremendous problems in their marriage. There were constant arguments and heated exchanges. The husband complained that his wife would "blow up" over the simplest of situations and refused to honor his leadership in the home. After numerous counseling sessions their marriage only grew worse. The case was referred to me and after further investigation; I discovered that she had been verbally abused by her father. She had never forgiven her father, and as a result, hatred of males developed in her heart. This left the door wide open for demonic spirits of hatred to control her behavior.

It would have been misguided of me to continue counseling the couple simply trying to resolve recurring strife. This type of dilemma required that the wife forgive her father and close the door to the spirits of hatred and unforgiveness in her life. This is a good reason why a counselor must be an individual who has the discerning of spirits operating in his life. In a situation like this, a mere surface investigation would yield very poor results. Only the fruit (the strife) would be detected and the root (unforgiveness and demonic influence) would remain in the ground. Demonic spirits must be discerned and dislodged through the power of the Holy Spirit.

I remember a man that came to my wife and me complaining of his wife's numerous character faults including her poor discipline habits. My wife and I arranged counseling for the couple. After a thorough counseling session, we discovered that although the wife had some unpleasant discipline problems, a spirit of pride possessed the husband and this demonic spirit activated his complaints. Previous counseling sessions had not discerned this spirit and a tumultuous marriage was the result. A deliverance session brought almost immediate results. The couple had been separated for almost six months but after three counseling sessions they were able to reunite and reconcile. The marriage still needs a lot of work but with the demonic spirit dislodged, the marriage was definitely back on the road to growth and maturity.

Family Spirits

Another type of baggage spirit is when a husband or wife comes from a family that has been possessed with a certain type of demonic manifestation. A man may come from a family where the father was a philanderer, drunkard, abusive, grouchy, lethargic, or participated in the occult which includes Free Masonry. A woman may have come from a family where the mother was dominant, unsubmissive, sensual, prideful, etc.

Because the wife or husband may be unaware of demonic spirits that operated in their families, the demon can easily take up residence in the new relationship. The key to obtaining deliverance is recognizing the evil spirit and renouncing it. The husband must come to grips with his (father) adulterous generational past and renounce it. The women whose family history reveals sensuality or promiscuity must do the same. This means that there must be a willingness to turn away from that sin or demonic manifestation and completely renounce it as being wrong. If these spirits are not renounced and cast out, they will continue to wreak havoc on their marital relationship.

Spirits That Enter Through Being Unequally Yoked

The Bible admonishes the believer not to yoke himself together with unbelievers 2 Corinthians 6:14-18 Some interpret this to mean that a person should not marry a person who is not a Christian. However, this scripture covers all relationships. This means that a Christian person should never form close habitual relationships with unbelievers. One person is under the control of the devil, and the other under the control of the Lord.

And, as always, the Devil-the charmer-never immediately shows his hand. Before he puts his aces on the table, he pretends that he means no harm and has no hidden agenda. This fools the Christian who is lured into the relationship and then completely fleeced by the Devil when he gets them into the right position. Some Christian businessmen lose their savings and reputations when they partner with unbelievers. The same is true of the young lady who falls in love with the unregenerated sinner naively believing that she can change him after marriage. But after marriage, she finds that her knight in shining armor quickly morphs into a demon.

A married person must be careful of the friends and associations that he or she makes and avoid those that could adversely affect their own life or marriage. He or she should never form a close relationship with a man or woman, club or organization that participates in or is known for perversion and sinful activity. People who choose to ignore this warning become easy prey for demonic spirits. I remember a time when my wife was working for a particular organization that frequently held overseas parties and functions for those employees who were successful during the year.

However, the company almost never invited the spouses of the successful individuals. After the groups would return from these overseas parties, there would be numerous rumors of infidelity and sexual promiscuity. This does not mean that we should never work for these types of organizations, but we should be alert and careful not to fall into the traps of lust and infidelity.

Some would claim that only the weak would fall in these situations, but if we know that the enemy has sprung a trap, why knowingly walk into it? The Bible says, *"Wherefore let him that thinketh he standeth take heed lest he fall." (1 Corinthians 10:12)* The Christian is admonished to avoid even the very appearance of evil. Many businessmen and women have allowed the Devil to trick them into working too closely with the opposite sex and opening a door where he can operate the spirit of lust that eventually caused them to fall into sin. *"But every man his tempted, when he is drawn away of his own lust and enticed, then when lust is conceived, it bringeth forth sin: and sin, when it is finished bringeth forth death." (James 1:14-15)*

When companies and businesses invite or compel you to go on trips whether as rewards, educational or transactions be alert. Close uninterrupted and private times with a female or male should be avoided. When inducement trips are awarded, and staff fun days given, always ask if your wife or husband can come along; especially if the opposite sex will be present.

Do not play the hero; even the most spiritual man or women can be lured into sexual attraction. The Bible has shown from the beginning of creation the weakness of man/woman in this area. David, Solomon and Samson are just a few who fell prey to fatal attraction. When the Devil springs his trap in this area, disgrace and contempt is very hard to wipe away. This is why the Apostle Paul told the Corinthian Saints to flee fornication. Once the gate of sexual attraction opens, it's like an overflowing river and almost impossible to stop.

Spirits of Strife

Another constant battle that couples go through is that of strife: endless arguments and disputes that seemingly arise from nowhere. Sometimes conflict can bring growth and development to a marriage if it is handled correctly, but in a lot of cases, behind the scenes of a "blow up" is a demonic spirit whose aim is to create unforgiveness, division, and separation in a marriage. A conflict can be beneficial if specific areas of problems are identified and brought to light for calm and meaningful discussion and resolution.

For example, a husband constantly drops his clothing on the floor, does not clean up behind himself, and is crudely undisciplined in his hygiene. It would be emotionally injurious for a wife to 'hold this problem in' and not confront the situation. She should wait for a good opportunity to confront him about his unpleasant habits, rather than allow her emotional feeling to fester until it becomes unbearable and potentially explosive.

On the other hand, arguments and confrontation can become real nasty when they are tricks played on the mind by demonic spirits. For example, a husband comes home tired from work. He barges into the door his mind preoccupied and tired from a hectic day. He forgets to say a pleasant word to his wife who may have been working hard in the house all day. Then, noticing her in the kitchen, he asks her if the dinner is ready. The evil spirits then begin their sinister plot. They whisper to the wife, "See how ungrateful he is, you have been slaving in this house all day, he hasn't said a kind word and all he wants to do is fill his big gut." The unsuspecting wife then responds to her husband with disdain and contempt. "I have been working hard in this house all day and all you can ask is if your dinner is ready...get it yourself!"

The husband not knowing what is going on quickly complains about his hard day at work but to no avail. The explanations and assertions rapidly turn into a full-fledged quarrel resulting with hurtful words and unwarranted tones of voices. The end result is confusion and emotional wounds. The demons laugh in glee, they have fulfilled their mission. The marriage partners, if they are not mature, will harbor these hurts leading to bitterness, lack of communication, vindictiveness and eventual divorce. The marriage is off balance, and only forgiveness and godly wisdom can get it going again.

The only antidote for this scenario is 2 Corinthians 10:5 *"Casting down imaginations, and every high thing that exalteth itself against the knowledge of God, and bringing into captivity every thought to the obedience of Christ."* Flesh and willful behavior must die. Reject thoughts that exalt self and be willing to esteem the other better that oneself. Of course, the so-called psychologist would rush to than, "we must first love ourselves." "Keep your boundaries up." "Remember your lines of respect."

These statements may be true in some circumstances, especially when someone is ill-informed, ignorant of their responsibility, or falling down in performance of duties. However, Christianity calls for self-denial and a cross. This stops us from satisfying our own selfish desires and binds us to look beyond our mate's faults and see their needs.

This would hold the wife back from responding self-righteously (a position of, "I am right and you are wrong") to her husband who has overlooked her consistent hard work. She is "working as to the Lord." This would prevent a man from scolding his wife's non performance of some duties because "love suffereth long and is kind."

The key is recognizing that your mate is unaware that Satan is trying to get a foothold in the relationship. At this juncture you must cover them. *"And above all things have fervent charity among yourselves; For charity shall cover the multitude of sins." (1 Peter 4:8)* This is not an easy task because your flesh will cry out for vengeance, for recognition, and for appeasement. But your spiritual man (the voice the Devil wants to drown out) will say, "forgive her, forgive him, they don't understand." When you forgive, you stop the spirit of bitterness from developing and defiling you. *"Follow peace with all men, and holiness, without which no man shall see the Lord: Looking diligently lest any man fail of the grace of God; lest any root of bitterness springing up trouble you, and thereby many be defiled; (Hebrew 12:14-15)* Unforgiveness is a spiritual defilement that causes hardness of the heart (bitterness, hatred, coldness) and prevents the believer from moving forward in Christ or having his prayers answered.

There are numerous ways that spirits enter marriages to cause havoc. However, your response will determine whether your marriage survives or dies. If you equip yourself through prayer and the word of God, you will be successful. When the Devil tried to deceive Jesus, he was met with the sword of the Spirit. Even on the cross, Jesus refused to allow the flesh to dominate him and asked God to forgive the people who crucified him. You must respond to the Devil in the same way. It's the only way to survive in our very dark time. It is also the way to life and victory.

4. Weapons that Work

A large number of *divorced people* claimed that they have tried everything to save their marriages, but nothing seems to have worked for them. They claim that they tried forgiveness, submission, love, and, patience but they still came up losers. Some were even told by counselors and spiritual leaders that their marriages were hopeless and a divorce was the only solution. I submit that all efforts tried without God's help and guidance will prove fruitless.

But those who give God the opportunity to work for them will indeed experience his grace and power. This is not a guarantee that their dilemma will be solved overnight, but it does mean that the power of the universe will be at their disposal. After Jesus arose from the dead, he told his disciples that all power was given to him in heaven and in earth. (Matthew 28:18) Yes, the greatest source of power in the universe is available to those who believe. And like the Bible says *"nothing is impossible to them that believe."*

After Paul told the Ephesians Saints of the great power that the church wields, and that he prays that God would open their minds to grasp this revelation, he ended this enlightening epistle by telling the Ephesians believers to Stand. *"Wherefore take unto you the whole armor of God that yea may be able to withstand in the evil day and having done all to stand. Stand therefore, having your loins girt about with truth and having on the breastplate of righteousness. And your feet shod with the preparation of the gospel of peace. Above all taking the shield of faith wherewith ye shall be able to quench all the fiery darts of the wicked. And take the helmet of salvation and the sword of the Spirit which is the word of God. Praying always with all prayer and supplication in the Spirit and watching thereunto with all perseverance and supplication for all saints;..."* (*Ephesians 6:13-18*)

Learning how to defend yourself and to appropriate the victory at Calvary is your key to success in this marriage warfare. You are not fighting from a position of weakness or inferiority. Jesus said that the gates of hell would never prevail against you. *"And I say also unto thee,*

That thou art Peter, and upon this rock I will build my church and the gates of hell shall not prevail against it." (Matthew 16:18) But ignorance of the proper use of our weapons can prove disastrous. The believer must play his part in this spiritual battle. God wants the believer to use the weapons that He has provided to vanquish the enemy and enforce the victory at Calvary.

First, saturate your marriage life with prayer. Prayer changes things. Prayer moves the hand of God. James 5:17-18 states, *"Elias was a man subject to like passions as we are and he prayed earnestly that it might not rain; and it rained not on the earth by the space of three years and six months. And he prayed again, and the heaven gave rain, and the earth brought forth her fruit."* Reading, studying, attending conferences are good but if you never pray; the power to change things and to destroy the strongholds of Satan are negated. Ask God for wisdom and revelation in closing spiritual doors in your life, and the life of your spouse that are open to the enemy.

Spend time in your prayer closet. Spend time in prayer and bible study with your spouse and family. And at times, combine prayer with fasting to bring down those strongholds in your life and in your spouse's life. Jesus told his disciples to watch and pray. (Matthew 14:38) This is one of the prime reasons that many lose before the fight even begins. They have not prayed for God's guidance. They have not asked for his protection. They have not yielded their lives to God. Monday Night prayer meeting is said to be one of the most sparsely attended services on the church calendar, could this be another reason for many losing the war to save their marriages?

The Apostle Peter warns the believer *"But the end of all things is at hand: be ye sober, and watch unto prayer." (1 Peter 4:7)* The battle is not going to get easier. Therefore, we must step up our spiritual activity. We must pray and seek God like never before. Don't be deterred by what others are doing. Turn off the TV and pray! Pull away from the Internet and chat rooms and pray.

Use The Word To Protect Your Marriage

Speak the word over your marriage. Usually, when people are going through trying situations in their marriage, negative advice is always forthcoming; advice that is in conflict with the word of God. "Child, you don't have to stay in that marriage." "Girl if I were you, I would get rid of him." "Boy, that's women these days, don't put up with it." But the word of God says, *"What therefore God has joined together, let not man put asunder." (Matthew 19:6)*

Use the same weapon that Jesus used against the Devil when he was tempted Jesus: The Word of God. Even when things get difficult continue to use the sword of the spirit. *"And we know that all things work together for good to them that love the Lord, and to them who are called according to his purpose." (Romans 8:28)*

The Devil would like for you to speak and receive negative words about your mate and your marriage. This is what the Apostle Peter was talking about in 1 Peter 3:9 *"Not rendering evil for evil or railing for railing: but contrariwise blessing knowing that ye are there unto called that ye should inherit a blessing."* Remember you will have what you say. Life and death are in the power of the tongue. Insulting words, faultfinding, and belittling only add fuel to the Devil's fire. Words of encouragement, words of love are the glue that holds are for the marriage together and the fertilizer that helps marriages to grow. Even when things go wrong - and they will - don't give in to your flesh. Build your relationship, don't break it down. Proverbs 15:1 states that a soft answer turns away wrath but grievous words stirs up strife.

Learn to forgive your spouse unconditionally. Peter asked Jesus if one should forgive his brother at least seven times. However, Jesus replied that as long as a person is truly repentant, he should be forgiven. *"Until seven times seventy seven." (Matthew 18:21)* Sadly, today sin is categorized in the marriage relationship. To some sexual sins are unpardonable, and only minor infractions are to be forgiven. But sin is sin! Yes, some are indeed more grievous than others, and some cause more damage than others. The truth is, however, we all owe God so much that we cannot afford to be unforgiving or hold a grudge against someone else. (Matthew 18:23-35)

When You Lose a Skirmish

In every war, there are times when it seems that the enemy is gaining ground. There may even be times when the enemy may seem to have won a skirmish. Don't allow this to detour you. For example, you lose your temper. You said something insulting to your mate. You started divorce proceeding. Do what Peter did when he denied the Lord. Repent! Don't delay! Proverbs 6:2 says, *"Thou art snared with the words of thy mouth, thus art taken with the words of thy mouth. Do this now, my son, and deliver thyself, when thou art come into the hand of thy fried; go, humble thyself, and make sure thy friend. Give not sleep to thine eyes, nor slumber to thine eyelid. Deliver thyself as a roe from the hand of the hunter, and as a bird from the hand of the fowler."* A quick apology will neutralize the Devil's ability to develop unforgiveness and bitterness in the heart of your mate.

Don't brood over past failure. Brooding over past failures is a sign of pride. Accept them as learning experiences and as stepping-stones to a higher plateau of marital maturity. Even your mistake is in God's plan. Sometime a failure may reveal an area that needs more prayer. Sometimes a failure brings humility and a deeper sense of need for God's grace. Whatever the circumstances, stay focused, and keep your eyes on Jesus who is the author and finisher of your faith.

Here are just a few scriptures to encourage and use against the enemy attacks.

Assurance of Salvation

"And they said, Believe on the Lord Jesus Christ, and thou shalt be saved and thy house." (Acts 16:31)

"There hath no temptation taken you but such as is common to man: but God is faithful, who will not suffer you to be tempted above that ye are able; but with the temptation also make a way to escape, that ye may be able to bear it." (1 Corinthians 10:13)

Blessings

"Blessed is every one that feareth the Lord; that walketh in his ways. For thou shalt eat the labour of thine hand: happy shalt thou be, and it shall be well with thee. Thy wife shall be as fruitful vine by the sides of thine house: thy children like olive plants round about thy table." (Psalm 128:1-3)

"And it shall come to pass, if thou shall hearken diligently unto the voice of the Lord thy God to observe and to do all his commandments which I command thee this day that the Lord thy God will set thee on high above all nations of the earth. And all these blessing shall come on thee and overtake thee, if thou shall hearken unto the voice of the Lord thy God. Blessed shalt thou be in the city, and blessed shalt thou be in the field." (Deuteronomy 28:1-3)

"Now unto him that is able to do exceeding abundantly above all that we ask or think according to the power that worketh in us." (Ephesians 3:20)

"Blessed be God even the Father of our Lord Jesus Christ the Father of mercies, and the God of all comfort; who comforteth us in all our tribulation that we may be able to comfort them which are in any trouble by the comfort wherewith we ourselves are comforted of God." (2 Corinthians 1:3-4)

"We are troubled on every side, yet not distressed: we any perplexed, but not in despair, Persecuted, but not forsaken; cast down but not destroyed." (2 Corinthians 4:8-9)

Assurance of Victory

"There hath no temptation taken you but such as is common to man: but God is faithful, who will not suffer you to be tempted above that ye are able; but will with the temptation also make a way to escape, that ye may be able to bear it." (1 Corinthians 10:13)

"Nay, in all these things we are more than conquerors through him that loved us. For I am persuaded that neither death nor life, nor angels, nor principalities, nor powers, nor things present, nor things to come, Nor height, nor depth, nor any other creature, shall be able to separate us from the love of God, which is in Christ Jesus our Lord." (Romans 8:37-39)

In Need of Encouragement

"Wait on the Lord: be of good courage and he shall strengthen thy heart, wait I say on the Lord." (Psalm 27:14)

"And he saith unto me, My grace is sufficient for thee: for my strength is made perfect in weakness. Most gladly therefore will I rather glory in my infirmities, that the power of Christ may rest upon me." (2 Corinthian 12:9)

In Need of Protection

"The angel of the Lord encampeth around them that fear him, and delivereth them." (Psalm 34:7)

Hopeless Situation

"The righteous cry, and the Lord heareth, and delivereth them out of all their troubles. The Lord is nigh unto them that are of a broken heart; and saveth such as be of a contrite spirit. Many are the afflictions of the righteous: but the Lord delivereth him out of them all." (Psalm 34:17-18)

5. Making Reconciliation Work

Over and over again, we hear the story about how Karen and Michael got back together, but it only lasted a few weeks, months, or years, and eventually the marriage was dissolved or they became separated again. Then comes the nagging questions: Why didn't the marriage work if they were trying? Why couldn't they surmount the difficulties that they were facing? Who was to blame? Are most marriages just destined to be this way? Can reconciliation really work, or giving up simply the best thing to do?

The reality behind these questions may not be obvious to you, but the truth will motivate you to believe in hope and to survive when all else is saying give up. Yes, God is still sovereign! Man always creates problems for himself but his biggest failure is trying to solve his problems without Christ as his helper. Jesus told his disciples that *"without me ye can do nothing."* Keeping Christ as the center of our lives has always been the struggle that keeps most people from achieving God's blessings. For those who reconcile this is usually their failing. Remaining focused when the enemy returns to cut the cords of recovery. The Devil will return to aggravate the pain, rekindle the strife, and evoke the shocking memories. But you must not be daunted nor retreat in fear. Stay focused!

Several years ago, I visited a friend who became a Christian shortly after his marriage had failed. When I met him, he was still bitter toward his wife for the many humiliating things that she had put him through. He was determined to divorce his wife and remain single, but after much prayer and encouragement, he decided to reconcile with his estranged wife. She had at that time, been in a very serious accident and was hospitalized. He asked me to visit and pray with her. I did as he asked me to and visited her in the hospital. When I talked with her, she resisted the idea of reconciliation with her husband, but after just a few words of prayer, the power of God fell, and she burst into tears confessing, and repenting.

After she got out of the hospital, she returned to her husband, and for a few months every thing seemed all right. But after only a year, they again separated. Afterwards, I asked Andrew (not his real name) what happened, didn't God bring them together for keeps? He said that after they got back together, "things were so good that he stopped going to church and reading his Bible and the merry-go-around of strife and bickering started all over again." After that, it was only a matter of time before they could not live together and separation was the only means of preserving peace and sanity.

I want to share something with you that will revolutionize your thinking about marriage and your Christian theology. Again, your problem is not your mate; you must look beyond their faults and inconsistencies. Even beyond that crafty Devil and his subtle devices. You must allow the Holy Spirit to crucify and deaden the place that Satan is always looking for, your flesh: that willful, impatient, prideful, and selfish nature that resides in every man. If this is crucified, then living with your mate, regardless of his or her faults, would be a piece of cake! This is one of the main reasons reconciliation fail. Partners allow the enemy to aggravate that un-crucified area. And they fall back into the same sins that caused the break-up in the first place.

The flesh is very subtle and when you believe you have it under control, it springs up seemingly from nowhere. You thought you had overcome that unbridled sexual desire, or the accusatory spirit. You thought that you had banished that stubborn nature or prideful attitude only to find them dominating your flesh all over again. The Apostle Paul says, *"Wherefore seeing we also are compassed about with so great a cloud of witnesses, let us lay aside every weight, and the sin which doth so easily beset us, and let us run with patience the race that is set before us, Looking unto Jesus the author and finisher of our faith; who for the joy that was set before him endured the cross, despising the shame, and is set down at the right hand of the throne of God. For consider him that endured such contradiction of sinners against himself, lest ye be wearied and faint in you minds." (Hebrews 12:1-3)*

Our only defense against slipping into the flesh is constant obedience to the Spirit. We must humble ourselves before him and allow him to guide us through these sometime treacherous seas. *"This I say then, Walk in the Spirit, and ye shall not fulfill the lust of the flesh, For the flesh lusteth against the Spirit, and the Spirit against the flesh; and these are contrary the one to the other: so that ye cannot do the things that ye would."* (*Galatians 5:16-17*) The above story about Andrew and Sandra illustrate this fact. Who brought them back together? The Spirit of God. Who can keep them together? The Spirit of God. They separated again because they allowed the wrong spirit to come back into the marriage.

You must guard your reconciliation. Don't allow the Devil to bring offense and unforgiveness back into your marriage. The Devil is very agitated that your marriage is back together, and he will try anything to get the roots of bitterness and hatred to grow again. He will constantly maneuver to get you or you mate to act in a manner that caused the first break-up. "Watch out" it will come. But you must not be alarmed, it's only a mirage. God is still in control and Satan is grasping at straws trying to stop God's blessing on your marriage.

Reconciliation done too hastily is another reason why reconciliation may fail. Before sufficient healing has taken place, people run back in each other arms believing that the romance that they feel will overcome the challenges that they face. But when the pedal is put to the metal, they find that they can not outrun the storm. Their reconciliation fails and they separate, believing that marriage just can't work. However, in reconciliation as in all spiritual things, God's timing is everything. *"He hath made every thing beautiful in his time: also he hath set the world in their heart, so that no man can find out the work that God maketh from the beginning to the end."* (*Ecclesiastes 3:11*)

Never jump back into broken marriage until you have been given confirmation that it is time to return. This doesn't mean that since you go back under the backing of the Spirit that you won't have any problems. However, if we wait on God's timing, the Holy Spirit can complete the healing or discipline in a spouse's life that can make the reconciliation work. Also, there are some people who need counseling and spiritual growth before they can reconcile. If they reconcile before God's due date, the reconciliation will eventually fizzle out, and further attempts at reconciliation will be even that much harder.

Some people ask if there are marriages that just won't work. Sure! But statistics prove that most marriages are salvageable and manageable (98% according to most counselors) if we are willing to put our willful and selfish attitudes behind us. Marriage requires hard work. You have to work at it! There is no other way. Admittedly, there are a very small percentage of marriages where a lifetime separation may be best for both partners; a path that should be chosen only after receiving confirmation from the Holy Spirit that this is God's will.

This book is not intended to be a panacea for marriage problems. Nor is it an attempt to blame the Devil for all our marital ills; some problems can be solved by a simple attitude adjustment, and others by taming the flesh through fasting and prayer. But suffice it to say, as long as we live, there will be problems that marriages will have to face. The intent of this book is to uplift and encourage couples to fight scripturally for their marriages. Jesus's defense to the Devil was always, *"it is written."* He was successful. Those who want to be successful must also use this same method, *"It is written."*

I would like to close with a page from world boxing history. It was dubbed the greatest fight ever. The smart talking and quick jabbing former champion Mohammed Ali had gained a World Title Fight with the most devastating fighter of all time. George Foreman was a man with unnatural strength. Up to that point, he had literally pulverized all his opponents, and Ali was to be just another one on his list. Most people counted Ali out. Although he had been a former champion with exceptional boxing skills, they considered him breakfast for the powerful Foreman.

But Ali was undaunted, he promised the public that Foreman would fall and he would be the champion. By then, Ali had embarked upon a new style of boxing called the "rope-a-dope." Because he was not as energetic as in his younger years, he decided that he would conserve his energy early in the fights by covering up his upper body, and allowing the other fighters to wear themselves out by punching him in the stomach. When his opponents tired, Ali would come of the ropes using his punches with devastating speed and accuracy.

Finally, the day came and Ali and Foreman met in their scheduled fourteen rounder. In the early rounds, Foreman seemed to have the fight won. He punched Ali about the body with hard resounding blows. In the second round, he rocked Ali with a devastating punch to the head. Onlookers expected the fight to end in round three. But Ali hung on. He constantly tied up Foreman frustrating his knockout attempts. Slowly, as Foreman tired, Ali came off the ropes and began to fight. Zip, bang, bop, Ali connected with Foreman's head with ferocious speed and deadly accuracy. The "rope-a-dope" paid off! Then in the eighth round, Ali went in for the kill. He caught Foreman with a left right combination and the Fat Lady sang her tune. It was all over! Ali was Heavyweight Champion of the World!

Dear friend, you might be on the ropes, you may be down for the count. Your situation may look dim; your husband may be in the arms of his lover. Your finances may be a mess. You may have just gotten your divorce papers. Don't give up! Don't waste your time in a pity party or in vengefulness. Don't splatter your business on Divorce Court. Do the rope-a-dope! Save your energy and grab hold of the mighty shield of faith that is able to quench the many darts of the enemy. Then come off the ropes and fight! Heaven is on your side, and greater is he that is in you than he that is in the world!

A Prayer for Deliverance and Protection

Father, I thank you for your grace and mercy. Thank you for the precious blood of Jesus that was shed for me at Calvary. Father, I praise you, the great God who is the source of all power and life. Today, I bring my marriage problem/situation to you. I recognize that of myself, I can do nothing but through you I can do all things. I put my marriage into your hands. I request your wisdom and guidance. Father, I submit myself to you, and ask for your grace to walk in my marriage according to your word.

I plead the blood of Jesus Christ over my marriage. My marriage belongs to You. I rebuke every foul spirit. I renounce every demonic spirit that has entered my marriage _____ (call the names i.e.. pride, confusion, infidelity, domination, abuse etc.) I take authority over every demon of _____ (call the names of the spirits that have been affecting your marriage.) I command these demons _____ (names) to leave in the name of Jesus Christ. Father, give me guidance to protect my deliverance and close the doors in my life that might be open to Satan's entrance and deception. Help me to change attitudes and to renew my mind through your word.

Father, I recognize that my husband/wife has a will of his/her own, but I stand upon your word that you will save me and my household. I plead the blood of Jesus Christ over his/her life and ask you to intervene on my behalf. Father, bring conviction, bring understanding, bring wisdom, bring love into his/her life in abundance. Only you know the heart of all man, only you can change the heart of man. You have said that if I abide in you and if your words abide in me, I can ask what I will and it shall be done unto me. I ask for you to bring a change in the life of my wife/husband.

Thank you for fulfilling your word. Thank you for hearing my prayers. Thank you for grace to wait patiently for the manifestation in the realm of the physical. Amen.

Part Two
Understanding Male Authority

Introduction

The keys to divine authority have been lost in our apostate times. Most men are in a coma, knocked out in the tenth round by a clever and superior opponent. However, all is not lost. The Lord is still calling!!

Like the day Adam lost authority in the Garden of Eden, the Lord is calling men back to Him; back to a place where they can find *real* power and wisdom to overcome their most elusive foe.

For men to recover what they have lost, they must undress. They must shed the garments of pride and arrogance. They must return to the Master's feet and learn. My prayer for every man that reads this section is true repentance. The Lord has not changed. We have.

We have turned from grace and mercy to do our own thing. Now, the enemy has gained the edge and our only hope is the Lord. Our only hope is to uncover the forgotten principles that bring God's grace. As you turn the pages of this section, let the mercy and grace of God open you eyes to see and understand truth that would usher you into a new realm of authority.

6. The Awakening

The siren was blaring in my ears. I was sitting beside the pastor's wife who was telling me that everything was going to be okay. But why was I in the back of an ambulance? And who was the bloodied white male lying motionless and breathing heavily under the oxygen mask? *"Brother Sands....your car collided with his."* Turning to the man, whom I had never seen before, I prayed for him. It was a reflective action. I was in a daze and operating in auto-mode. "Did I get married?" Sister Alleyne smiled but didn't reply. She rubbed my shoulder instead.

When the ambulance reached the hospital, I was quickly ushered into an emergency room. "How many fingers do I have up?" "Three", I replied. "And what year is it?" "I honestly don't know," I replied. The doctor had a concerned look on his face as he pressed heavily on several parts on my body asking if I felt pain. "No, just my arm hurts a little." After further examination, the doctor sounded relieved to tell me that I was okay and I could go home but I should be monitored for any change.

I was happy to know my good prognosis, but I had lost almost a year of information! I was suffering from temporary amnesia. The accident had knocked information out of my head. I had only been married a month. That information was gone. I knew Kim (my wife) but I couldn't remember that we were married. That night we slept in the same bed...in faith!

If you have never experienced amnesia, you won't understand this experience. You just can't remember "stuff". You can't connect to facts that are supposed to be in your memory bank. **Information and facts can be staring you right in the face and you cannot comprehend them.** You are in a trance unable to properly relate to what is happening. Wow! Today, sad to say, most men are in this predicament: In a deep sleep, unable to respond properly to what is happening around them.

A cunning and crafty enemy has knocked us into a coma. And, before we can assume our God-called position, we must understand who we are, and what we are called to do. You see, we were created with awesome power and ability to rule the world. Power that was lost the day Adam sinned in Eden. It took me some time to get my memory back, and it will take time for men to understand and walk in their God ordained authority. It started in Eden, and that is where we must return to understand God's purpose for men and what went wrong.

Who Am I?

The hovering bright light was the first thing that Adam saw when he opened his eyes. The brilliant light enveloped his naked body, giving him alternating sensations of joy, peace and love. All at once, he knew who he was and why God had created him. His name was Adam and God had created him to govern the Earth. Lying down on the ground, spiritual knowledge flowed through his mind and heart like a rushing river cascading over banks of a high fall. He was aware of God and the world that God had created for him.

The days and weeks after his creation, Adam's spiritual growth progressed unabated. Daily, God would visit him and commune with him, spiritually empowering him with divine knowledge to govern his environment. God continued to assign him more duties. First, he was given the chore of keeping and dressing of Eden. Then, he was given the task of naming the animals. Everything seemed to be going well and God was pleased with his progress.

Now, Adam was ready for his final test of authority. God had placed within Adam at creation, a rib, female DNA that would soon be his wife, the best thing that he could ever have. Then the day finally came. While Adam was asleep under the anesthesia of the Holy Spirit, God surgically removed the embryo DNA and made Eve. Together, they were to govern the earth. It was pure ecstasy for both of them as they played and romanced inside the confines of Eden. Little did they know that in a few months, they would be kicked out of their garden paradise and introduced to a life of pain and suffering.

The Bible says that God created man (meaning mankind) in His own image and likeness. Both male and female represent the invisible

God. Genesis 1:27 "So God created <u>man (mankind) in his own image</u>, in the image of God created he him; male and female created he them." For those who thought that God is a man, (meaning male man)...think again. God is neither a male nor a female. **He is a spirit.** However, He has chosen to reveal His attributes *differently* through the male and female gender. The purpose of this book is to isolate the male role or male side of God as best as I can.

Adam, the male, was created first. This is significant. He was created first for a specific purpose. He was the one designated with senior authority and leadership. Thus, he became ***responsible*** for the spiritual atmosphere of the whole world. The days and weeks before Eve was created were for the sole purpose of education; he needed to understand and flow in his role, or better, let God flow through him. God did this by assigning him tasks. He was to be a caretaker of the Garden of Eden. We don't know exactly what that entailed, however, when God cursed the ground, He said, *"...thorns also and thistles shall it bring forth to thee; and thou shalt eat the herb of the field." (Genesis 3:18)*. From this we can surmise that Adam's task may have included landscaping and gardening.

He was also given the task of naming the animals *and even eventually named his wife*. But, how did he learn to do all this? Did it just come to him? Did he rationalize and came to a conclusion about what to do? No, and a million times no. Adam was created pure, meaning without sin. **When Adam came off the product line God could freely fellowship with him.** This is an awesome statement!!

You see, God is authority and the source of every power behind the universe. God also has all knowledge and all wisdom. God is behind nature. He is behind gravity and every other law that we use to gauge and measure the universe with. In fact, He holds everything together by His word. When He created man, He created him to walk in this authority. Wow! And Adam did just that. The wisdom of God flowed through Adam like a river. He understood how to take care of Eden. He knew what to call the animals. Don't the names lions, tiger, dog, eagle, raven, dove fit the creatures more than sophisticated scientific names like *Felis Concolor* – a mountain lion or *Castor Canadensisor* – a beaver?

My brother, God has designated you to walk in divine authority. He wants you to walk in the supernatural to sense his voice and know what He wants you to do. **This is your purpose: To use authority to uphold all that is good.** This is the authority that Adam gave up when he sinned. **This is the authority Satan resists.** He knows if you truly understand who you are, and the authority that God has made available to you, his goose is cooked in your life. When a man walks in authority, he can bring deliverance to his family.

When a man walks in divine authority, the wisdom of God is made available to him. He becomes a better lover to his wife because he understands her feminine needs. He sees through the cloud of human behavior and can make wise decisions based not on mere rational thought, but according to the wisdom of God's Spirit, which, by the way, is usually contrary to human thought. *Proverbs 3:6-7 "Trust in the LORD with all thine heart; and lean not unto thine own understanding. In all thy ways acknowledge him, and he shall direct thy paths. Be not wise in thine own eyes: fear the LORD, and depart from evil."*

Authority Lost

When Adam disobeyed the voice of God by eating from the fruit of Good and Evil, he aligned himself with Satan: the spirit of rebellion or the **my-way** spirit. Adam compromised his position of authority by following his wife in rebellion against the word of God. He compromised his authority to appease his wife. Indeed, it takes faith and confidence to obey the word of God when everybody else is doing their own thing. It's easy to suck up to people so we are not the odd one out. **But compromise is the spirit of the coward who is fearful and afraid to tackle and confront challenges.**

Always, and in every way, the question will be: Will we obey the word of faith or continue to take matters into our own hands? Will we listen to the voice of God or be dominated by our fears. The first sin was compromise and fear of rejection, which leads to selfish, self-centered decisions. Adam chose himself over loving God, and fear of losing Eve over gaining God's approval. For a moment, just a moment, Adam forgot who he was and what his purpose was. *He allowed Satan to cause him to give up his authority through compromise.*

This is the deadly sin that plagues most men; leaders and all who must bear the burden of responsibility. Will they compromise to appease or will they stand for the truth of God? Will they use the authority for selfish means or will they use their authority to further the plans of Almighty God? You see, authority is God's means of establishing order, keeping peace and fulfilling His will. Whether it is within the family or a nation, God uses authority to fulfill His will. Thus, God commissioned Adam to "keep" the garden. He was to use his authority to fulfill God's purposes.

This deadly sin of compromise can be seen throughout the Bible, where men instead of standing in authority in obedience to God, compromised for one reason or another to please either their own flesh or the flesh of others: whether it was wife, children, friends or countrymen. However, their sin not only affected them but their families and their nations. For Adam, his sin affected mankind. He was the first representative of God's authority on earth. And what he did, would determine the fate of mankind. Whether a life of perpetual peace, harmony, and physical abundance, or sorrow, pain, and labor.

The Hiding Place

Adam failed God's highest hope for mankind. However, he compounded the predicament in which he found himself by hiding. He *misunderstood* the heart of God and hid himself from the only person who could help him. This is now the tragedy of fallen mankind and the male man. He refuses to go to God. *He refuses to submit to the Lord's authority and spends his entire life making mistake after mistake.* You see, God has a will for mankind. He has a will for every man and woman on the planet. And just as the angels in heaven fulfill His every purpose, His perfect plan is for every man and woman to daily do the same.

When we hide from our mistakes or from taking authority, it means that we are not properly connected to the source and we cannot see spiritually to make the right decisions. Like Adam, who was afraid to approach God after he had sinned, when we live far from God, we are unsure of His intentions or his plans for us. We believe the lies of Satan and his cohorts. Sadly, most men live in this insecurity and fear that cause them to shrink back from standing up to the deceptions of Satan.

Defeated men put on a mask of pride or false sense of strength to cover their fears and insecurities. They pretend that they have it all together but when they are put to the test, they compromise. Story after story is told in the Bible of men, who instead of standing in their position of authority, compromised to appease others.

Adam, Abraham, Lot, Saul, Eli the priest, all tasted the sour grapes of appeasement. They disobeyed God's word and His revelation to them to please someone else. In each case, instead of referring to God and what God said, they listened to the subtle and rebellious voice of self; the area where Satan controls and hides in our lives.

Abraham's mistake is a classic example of compromise. After years of no children, his wife, Sarah, decided to help God succeed. She told Abraham to copulate with her maid, Hagar, and, thus, they would fulfill the plan of God. Abraham, instead of asking God's opinion through prayer and waiting on God's reply went ahead. Abraham got his son, Ishmael, but this was not God's choice. Alas, this man-made plan would not cause only cause Abraham heartache when he had to send Ishmael away when Isaac, the child of promise, was eventually born. This man-made plan brought hatred, envy, and eventually war between the Jews and the ancestors of Ishmael which exists even to this day!

We must never hide or disengage ourselves from taking or standing in our position of righteous authority in our homes, or wherever we have been given a position of authority. If we fail to do this and do something else, his is called compromise. It brought death to the human race then and will continue to bring death and destruction until men and those who hold authority stand for truth and justice. The world itself is in the grip of fear and insecurity. Goliath looks to strong. Facing the mountain of fear looks impossible. But I'm here to tell every man that all the power in the universe is waiting to be released into your spirit. The door is now open for all who want to walk in true authority. All it takes is a willing and obedient spirit.

Hiding means fear and insecurity. Adam hid because he was not sure whether God would accept him back as a friend after he had sinned. He did not know God well enough to understand the heart of a father who only wants the son to acknowledge his sin and total dependency on the father. Yes, there would be consequences for his mistake. *However, God still wanted to fellowship with him and would one day die for this "sin" of mankind.*

7. Walking in Divine Authority

In 1991, my wife and I moved into our new home. We had lived in an apartment after we got married and this was a welcomed change. We were overjoyed over this latest accomplishment. However, shortly thereafter, the strife and bickering started: arguments about finances and who is really in charge, and as usual I pulled rank. "I'm the man around here and you do what I tell you...." But that only escalated the conflicts. One day after a heated exchange, I went into the bedroom and prayed one of the strangest prayers. Looking back, I know it had to be... the Holy Ghost.

I confessed before God that I was the blame, and took full responsibility. I wept before him and asked his forgiveness and direction. Shortly after I had finished praying, my wife came into the bedroom. She was different, her attitude of defiance was gone, and from that moment I knew that our marriage would survive this hump. But what had brought about this sudden change? And would it continue?

Like I said, I didn't know why I prayed as I did. Apparently, God had stepped in my prayer life and even in my ignorance, helped me. You see, our problems are never with just humans alone. Our real enemy is Satan, the God of this world. He is the deceiver. He is the marriage destroyer. He is the resister of truth and justice. Jesus said that the thief cometh to kill, steal and destroy but I have come to bring life. Without the wisdom of God, Satan can outfox and outmaneuver us. Like Jesus, who always walked in victory, we must depend completely on the Holy Spirit.

When I argued with my wife, I was depending on self. It was pride that made me say, "I'm the man." *"Only by pride cometh contention: but with the well advised is wisdom." (Proverbs 13:10)* For most men, we have been brought up in a society that glorifies pride (the devil's world). A society that tells us that being the first and the best is life's aim. A society that says that being superior is right. But, when we move in pride, we move further and further away from the power and wisdom of God.

However, like I related in my personal experience, as I yielded myself to God, there was a divine flow of authority, and there was an immediate change in my home. Humility is one of the greatest demonstrations of faith. *When a person humbles himself before God, he becomes a candidate for God's awesome power.* "*If my people which are called by my name, shall humble themselves and pray, and seek my face, and turn from their wicked ways; then will I hear from heaven, and will forgive their sin, and will heal their land.*" (2 Chronicles 7:14) "*Humble yourselves therefore under he mighty hand of God, that he may exalt you in due time:* (1 Peter 5:6) "*When pride cometh, then cometh shame: but with the lowly is wisdom.*" (Proverbs 11:2)

Humility is the key to divine authority, and the key to heavenly resources. It's the missing dimension in the lives of most men (and most people in general) as they struggle through life making prideful, arrogant, and self-centered decisions. In contrast, the door of humility looks plain; it looks drab, it looks forbidden and uninviting; but it is the only way to the favor of God and power of God. It is the key to truly walking in the awesome position of masculine authority. The power of God, the power that can move mountains, is activated by humility. "*The sacrifices of God are a broken spirit: a broken and a contrite heart, O God, thou wilt not despise.*" (Psalm 51:17) "*For all those things hath mine hand made, and all those things have been, saith the LORD: but to this man will I look, even to him that is poor and of a contrite spirit, and trembleth at my word.*" (Isaiah 66:2)

Humility is like a giant magnet that draws the awesome power of God. Most families today are struggling because husbands and fathers are walking in pride. Without genuine humility and keen spiritual insight, most men cannot flow in the blessing of God.

But what does humility really look like? Is it the spirit of the dutiful or go-for man that obeys the every whim of his wife and kids? Is it the self-righteous spirit that does all the good moral things? Again, we have to go back to the perfect image of Christ. What was he like? How did he portray humility? The Bible says that though He was the Son of God, *yet learned he obedience* by the things that He suffered (Hebrews

5). Humility is the maturity of submission and obedience. His every move, His being, was simply to please God; not people, not religious traditions, not His own will, but the will of the Father.

Humility means we are dedicated to God and empowered by the Holy Spirit. It calls for **sensitivity** and determination, gentleness and also confrontation. In Jesus, we saw tenderness but He preached fire and brimstone messages. We saw compassion, yet He sharply rebuked the religious leaders of His day. We saw a man run from the praise and accolades of people, yet one who was perfectly secure in who He was. In other words, humility cannot be manufactured; God has to produce humility in us as we learn to obey Him, even in the most trying circumstances.

This requires faith and patience, and an attitude that is totally dependent on God. God chooses our course, we ask Him for faith and patience to stay the course. The Bible says before honor there must be humility. However, for most men, the Devil has put up roadblocks in their minds about their authority. When they think of authority, they usually think of commanding power over people: To have people to obey their wishes and commands. This is not God's image of authority. God's authority is servant-hood and ministry. *"Ye know that the princes of the gentiles exercise dominion over them, and they that are great exercise authority upon them. But it shall not be so among you but whosoever will be great among you, let him be your minister. And whosoever will be chief among you, let him be your servant; Even as the Son of man came not to be ministered unto but to minister and to give his life a ransom for many."* (Matthew 20:25-28)

Another way of looking at this is recognizing that at best, your position of authority is transparent. Transparency means that the man acknowledges that his authority is delegated. His authority has been given in order that he can be an earthly conduit of God's power flow to his family. He is not the final authority, God is. Therefore, his leadership and authority must be tempered with godly meekness. Meekness does not mean that a man is passive. Meekness means that he is broken before God. He is like the powerful stallion that has been broken by its master, and responds to the faintest movement of the reigns. This is the epitome of true leadership and delegated authority.

Meekness was the trademark of great men like Abraham, Moses and the Lord himself who said, *"For I am meek and lowly..."* Without meekness leadership will degenerate into fleshly control and coercion. Meekness opens the door for the Spirit of God to direct the man. He can deny himself and allow God to channel through him, the flow of wisdom and spiritual perception that his family needs. The Apostle Paul discovered that when he was weak (weak in his own strength) he was most strong (2 Corinthians 12:8-10).

I remember a particular time, praying and asking God for wisdom to direct my home, and the Marriage Mechanics Ministries. Each time I prayed the Holy Spirit stopped me. I felt myself being constrained. Why, I questioned God? Was not this a valid prayer? God told me I did not understand; I was still thinking in the natural, I was still on the surface with regard to his manifold wisdom. But after a few days, he revealed his wisdom to me. "Its delegated authority, your authority comes through me. You must *allow the authority to flow through you*. You must allow me, to do the work through you. You must die to self. Self is that un-crucified area of your life that will use the authority for ungodly means."

You see, I was still thinking as a natural person thinks, that the wisdom and knowledge that they have is to be used as they deem fit. But God wants his people to die completely to self and allow him to channel his glory through them. The Apostle Paul puts it this way, *"I am crucified with Christ: nevertheless I live; yet not I, but Christ liveth in me: and the life which I now live in the flesh I live by the faith of the Son of God, who loved me, and gave himself for me."* (Galatians 2:20)

This is where men go wrong. This is where most leaders go wrong. They assume that since they have been appointed to a particular position that justifies their use of authority as they see fit. Or, God's anointing on my life justifies all of my decisions. This is not God's way. God's way is *"I and the Father are one."* (John 10:31) In other words, He flows through me unhindered. A man must learn that self-denial is not an option but his only way to true freedom and abundant flow in the spirit. He must learn to be quiet and allow the Spirit to speak through him. Then and only then would the words he speaks produce the powerful changes in his family that he desires.

Authority and the Wife

> *"And God said, Let us make man in our image, after our likeness: and let them have dominion over the fish of the sea, and over the fowl of the air, and over the cattle, and over all the earth, and over every creeping thin that creepeth upon the earth.*
>
> *So God created man in His own image, in the image of God created He him; male and female created He them." (Genesis 1:26-27)*
>
> *"And the Lord God said, It is not good that the man should be alone, I will make him an help meet for him." (Genesis 2:18)*
>
> *"And Adam gave names to all cattle, and to the fowl of the air, and to every beast of the field: but for Adam there was not found an help meet for him. And the Lord God caused a deep sleep to fall upon Adam, and he slept: and He took one of his ribs, and closed up the flesh instead thereof; And the rib, which the Lord God had taken from man, made he a woman, and brought her unto the man. And Adam said, This is now bone of my bones, and flesh of my flesh: she shall be called Woman Because she was taken of Man.*
>
> *Therefore shall a man leave his father and his mother, and shall cleave unto his wife: and they shall be one flesh. And they were both naked, the man and his wife, and were not ashamed." (Genesis 2:20-25)*

Before the fall, both man and woman were unified in their obedience to God. They walked in obedience and unity through the *empowerment of the Holy Spirit. The Holy Spirit was the key to their unity and relationship. This is God's perfect plan.* As we move forward toward the coming of the Lord, and His heavenly kingdom, the relationship between a husband and wife has to become more like God's perfect plan where the genders walk together in divine unity, both humbly doing His will. Let me explain.

It was never about exalting the man, or exalting the woman. It was always about doing God's will and displaying His masculine and feminine attributes. To God be all the glory forever and ever amen. Man and woman were created to glorify God. They were never to live for themselves, but to live to please Him, first. They did this before the fall.

However, after the fall, sin and rebellion entered the human race. Thus, mankind would now need external codes of ethics to govern their lives. God stated to the woman *"her desire would be to the husband and he would rule over her."* This was to keep her flesh in check, and punishment for overstepping God ordained authority, and not because she was any less or inferior to the man spiritually. Both man and woman are equal before God, however, there is, and always will be, order in God's kingdom.

God created your wife to be your helpmeet. This means she has been divinely created to assist you to fulfill your mission on earth. She has strengths where you are weak. Learn to listen to her advice especially in areas where you may be failing. Many men reap bitter results because they fail to listen. Contra wise, you can enjoy the blessing of a prudent wife *if you listen instead of trying to dominate and control her.*

Release her unto to the Lord and allow God to bring about the godly submission in her life. To demand or coerce you wife to submit to your authority, is not only counterproductive, it's ungodly and a gross exploitation of authority. Submission must be offered willingly. Have faith in God! He is very involved and interested in bringing divine order to your home, but it must be done His way: through the power of the Holy Spirit.

My wife and I were brought up in a very strict church background. The church that we attended taught against the wearing of jewelry as an ornament (Using 1 Timothy 2:9 and 1 Peter 3:3). However, over the years the "Jewelry For Ornament" teaching was revised and relaxed allowing members to wear jewelry in moderation. There was much confusion concerning the issue. I opted to stick to the old way. So every time my wife would put on jewelry, I would advise her against it. But daily I heard a voice within saying, "Release your wife, ...release your wife...." Finally, I obeyed and my wife started to wear the earring and bracelets. However, after several years of wearing, she confessed that indeed the Apostles' word concerning outward adornment was neither cultural nor contemporaneous to its time. She said that there was always a temptation to put on more and more. Now she has developed a discipline to keep the jewelry to a minimum.

Suppose I had not listened to the voice of the Holy Spirit. My wife would still be in bondage to law and would not come to the greater understanding of grace and wisdom through the power of the Holy Spirit. Let me give you another example, let's say you have requested your wife to do something for you, or she may be neglectful or derelict in performance of her duties as a wife. When you bring it to her attention, she resists you or fails to cooperate. Or, she may resist your decision on a certain financial matter. The fleshly and carnal response is usually anger or becoming argumentative. This only compounds the situation. The spiritual response, however, will bring the best result. Remain calm and continue to love. Remember God has everything under control. You must rely on him to show you the source of the problem. Could it be she doesn't understand or may be afraid of where the family is going? Take time to reassure her. Patiently wait for her to get the message or accept the idea you are trying to get across.

If she out-rightly defies you, let God handle the situation. Don't take matters into your own hands, this will prove devastating to your marriage. Always respond with love. Being a roughrider shows immaturity and insensitivity. Being right doesn't have to mean being harsh. There will be times and circumstances, when the Holy Spirit will direct you to move forward, regardless of your wife's wishes. However, be sensitive to her feelings and patient with her misunderstandings.

Are there times when a man must submit to his wife? In a technical sense, a man should never subject himself to his wife, this is totally contrary to God's word because the authority of God flows through him. However, a man must submit himself to the word of God and the Spirit of God. When his wife is in sync with God and operating under the influence of the Holy Spirit, a man would do well to heed her words. By doing so he demonstrates humility and the proper understanding of authority. She has been designed to help him. But this still does not change the position of husband or wife.

A good example of this can be seen in Genesis 21, when Sarah the godly wife of Abraham advised him to send away his son born to him by his mistress Hagar. Abraham was very distraught that his wife had asked him to do this and refused. But later he was told by God to hearken unto her voice. Why? She was speaking God's will. The key in these circumstances is to be so spiritually in tune that you can discern when one's wife is speaking God's word and giving good advice. Both men and women are required to obey God in everything. However, in the normal flow of authority in the home, a man is required to listen to his wife and to obey God. Conversely, a woman is required to obey her husband in everything. This does not mean that he sticks his wife in a small corner and runs the house himself. He should listen attentively to her suggestions and allow her to aid him.

Male authority was given for man to be a custodian of God's world. It was never given for man to create his own world. For a man to operate in the fullness of authority, man must submit himself unreservedly to Jesus Christ. When a man does this, he will find the power that created the universe. He will find the power that controls the atom. He will know God. God is power and authority.

8. Passivity: The Leadership Killer

I think one of the biggest mistakes that I have ever made was a result of my passivity. We were married almost ten years when Kim became pregnant with our fourth child. Before the baby was born, my wife suggested that she should have her fallopian tubes tied (Tubal Ligation). We had both come from families of four children, and it seemed the natural thing to have four of our own.

But the overwhelming reason for the Tubal Ligation was the anxiety and pride that we would look foolish and naïve having another child. At this time in our country, it was becoming a shame for a person even if they were married to have a large family. I loved my wife and I didn't want her to endure the constant anxiety and fear that she would become pregnant again, so I agreed to the Tubal Ligation.

Our obstetrician who had initially agreed to do the Tubal Ligation, later tried without success to dissuade us several times during our visits. He constantly cited that we were young and may change our minds in the future. He also reminded us that tragedy could also happen where we may lose a child and, as he explained it, a woman would always want a replacement. He recalled an incident with one of his patients that substantiated his point. However, we were determined to keep our family at four. I would live to regret my decision.

November in the Bahamas is weather paradise. The temperature hovers around seventy-five degrees with a soft delicate sea breeze. It's ideal for the outdoors and makes for a comforting time in the Bahamas after the summer heat. After work, Kim and headed home for eventful afternoon. It was not to be.

Shortly after we got home, Kim relieved our Jamaican maid.

> *"Miss Sands, I done feed*
> *the baybe and done burp*
> *her too.*
> *She was a good baybe*
> *today."*

With those few words, she was off to the bus stop. Kim went into the kitchen to prepare dinner and shortly afterward when to check our newborn.

The shrieking cry off my wife made me run to the bedroom.

"Lambert, the baby is not breathing!"

I went into fix-it mode.

"Kim, calm down. Let me see what I could do!"

Kimille's lifeless little body, arms dangling, made me want to cry but I had enough reserve fortitude to at least try CPR. When the ambulance arrived, we continued to try CPR on the way to the hospital to no avail.

At the hospital, the doctors tried without success to revive Kimille. She was gone...gone never to return. The pain that Kim and I endured over the next several weeks was unbearable. We both grieved in different ways. She wanted to share her grief by talking about it with me and others. I climbed into a spiritual hole just wanting the grief to go away.

It was only God's grace and mercy that pulled us through. One afternoon after work, we headed for the beach. The confrontation that we had wasn't easy but it eventually broke the down walls between us. Then the Lord stepped in and healed our hearts and our marriage. Shortly afterward, God birthed the Marriage Mechanics Ministries. To Him, we owe all the glory and praise!!

If we had prayed before we made our decision, I believe the outcome would have been different. My passivity opened the door for the enemy to bring bad advice. As a result, we reaped the results of our misguided decision. We must remember that when a man neglects or is ignorant of his leadership role, he leaves a void in his home.

In the spirit world, there are no vacuums. There is only God or the devil, good or evil. When a man is passive, it is usually the sign of a deeper spiritual problem. The enemy has a foothold in his life. **He has not acknowledged his position of authority** and has allowed the enemy to sidetrack him with the spirits of slothfulness, fear and stubbornness.

These are all negative forms of pride: *an unwillingness to confront problems and work through them.*

Positive pride is the false motivation that men feel when they are chasing the rainbow of success. Money, promotion and recognition take the place of a viable relationship with the Lord. Negative pride is the slothfulness and lethargy that men feel when they pamper themselves in fear or wallow in depression and inactivity. They avoid problems because they feel powerless and incapable. Eventually, the spirit of procrastination brings failure, debt and unnecessary burdens to the household. This leaves the wife frustrated, and in most cases anxious to assume leadership responsibility.

Modern males who growing up without a father figure in their lives are finding it more and more difficult to steer the head of the home position. Some are finding it difficult to provide adequately. Others are unsure which responsibilities are theirs and which are their wives'. The result is a passive uninformed man whose leadership is vulnerable to resistance and poverty. His laid-back attitude gives the devil a loophole to covertly operate a strategy of spoiling the vine with the little foxes.

Pathway to Dominion

"And God blessed them, and God said unto them, Be fruitful, and multiply, and replenish the earth, and subdue it: and have dominion over the fish of the sea, and over the fowl of the air, and over every living thing that moveth upon the earth. (Genesis 1:28)

"For as many as are led by the Spirit of God, thy are the sons of God." (Romans 8:14)

"Behold I give unto you power to tread on serpents and scorpions, and over a the power of the enemy: and nothing shall by any means hurt you." (Luke 10:19)

When God gave man the authority in the garden, He gave him the authority to have dominion. Dominion is translated from a Hebrew word "radah" and means: to tread down, subjugate, to crumble, to prevail against, to reign, and to rule. Man was commissioned by God as being the ruler and custodian over the earth. He was not just a mouthpiece saying that he was in control. Man was the god of this world. However, in the mechanics of his dominion, we must always remember the Holy Spirit.

Man's dominion was exhibited as he allowed the Holy Spirit to influence his actions and behavior. Adam would ensure that his garden tasks were accomplished before his scheduled meeting with God. He knew exactly what to name the animals. He knew how to talk and communicate with God. He knew what to name his wife. This was dominion.

Adam walked in complete faith and trust in God and his sinless nature was a riverbed for the flow of God's wisdom. But when Adam sinned, rebellion clogged up his spiritual arteries. Instead of operating in the depth of God's wisdom, he could use only ten percent of his brain. True story! He had to call on God to come and fill the void that was in his life. But it was never like it was before.

Although men of God like Solomon, Daniel and David demonstrated the wisdom of God, man's full restoration came when Jesus Christ went to Calvary and restored dominion back to man through His blood. God could reconnect with the spirit of man, forming a new man created in the image and likeness of God. *"Therefore if any man be in Christ, he is a new creature: old things are passed away; behold, all things are become new." (2 Corinthians 5:17)* Now, with Jesus Christ living within us, we have all the tools necessary to operate in dominion; the way God designed man to operate.

However, although man's spirit nature is reborn, he still lives in a fleshly body and his mind or soul needs renewal. Renewal comes as a man daily submits to the Holy Spirit who energizes the new man. This is why the Devil fights to confuse and obliterate the doctrines of the Blood of Jesus Christ, the Baptism of the Holy Spirit and walking in the Spirit. He knows that these doctrines are fundamental to achieving dominion. *"Howbeit when he, the Spirit of truth, is come, he will guide you into all truth, for he shall not speak of himself, but whatsoever he shall hear, that shall he speak: and he will shew you things to come." (John 16:13) "But ye shall receive power, after that the Holy Ghost is come upon you: and ye shall be witnesses unto me both in Jerusalem, and in all Judaea, and in Samaria, and unto the uttermost part of the earth." (Acts 1:8)*

When a person is renewed through the blood of Jesus Christ and the power of the Holy Spirit, they have been given dominion. They have been given authority to dominate every area of their lives. For a male man, God expects him to be excellent as head of the home. God doesn't want him to be a mediocre protector, God wants him to beat the devil up and kick him out of the family! God wants to make him a father of excellence and integrity. God wants to make him an able teacher by revealing divine secrets to him. God does not want him to be a lackadaisical provider; God wants him to be a man proficient with finances.

In most households, just the opposite is true. The average family is growing in debt. The devil is beating up men and kicking them out of their own homes. Children have become oppressors, and love life between husband and wife stinks! But I say to every man who is reading this book, your wife's happiness, your financial abundance, your children's salvation are wrapped up in you, and your authority in the home. You must exercise dominion by submitting yourself to the power of the Holy Spirit and faith in the finished work at Calvary.

Now I am going to give you a key that will unlock God's blessing upon your life. Faith. Wait a minute, you say, I have read about faith and I have practiced faith. I have preached faith. But I guarantee you, if you look back, in most cases, it was misguided faith; faith that was based on your own fleshly desires and expectations; the faith that most charismatic circles preach. Faith that causes people to be presumptuous and self-centered, believing that God is going to give them their every fleshly desire and bless their carnal decisions. God is not a genie. He is Lord and King, and we are His servants. He is the shepherd and we are the sheep. Yes, He has promised to meet our needs and "bless our socks off," but the promises are always conditional upon our obedience.

> *"And it shall come to pass, if thou shalt hearken diligently unto; the voice of the Lord thy God, to observe and to do all his commandments which I command thee this day, that the Lord thy God will set thee on high above all nations of the earth: And all these blessings shall come on thee, and overtake thee, if thou shalt hearken unto the voice of the Lord thy God."* (Deuteronomy 28:1-2)

God does not revolve around our needs and fancies. As we obey, we inherit our fortune. Consequently, real faith demonstrates self-denial, temperance, and unreserved obedience; hard to find in our so-called Christian society. For genuine dominion, we need God's faith; the faith that flows through you as you hear and obey the voice of God. Faith that sees what God sees. This is a different ball game! It takes time to achieve and develop. This is why Adam spent time learning from God before Eve was made. The reason why Paul spent time in Arabia before his ministry became prominent; the reason why Jesus ministry started at thirty instead of ten. They had to learn dominion. Let me give you an example. When God brought the people out of Egypt it was his purpose that they enter the Land of Promise. However, after forty years of meandering in the desert, they still did not enter. Why? Let God answer this one.

> *"Wherefore, (as the Holy Ghost saith, Today if ye will hear his voice, Harden not your hearts as in the provocation, in the day of temptation in the wilderness. When your fathers tempted me, proved me, and saw my works forty years. <u>Wherefore I was grieved with that generation, and said, They do always err in their heart; and they have not known my ways</u>. So I sware in my*

wrath, They shall not enter into my rest.) (Hebrews 3:7-11)

The people of God refused to exercise faith, although they had seen the demonstration of God's power. God wanted to take them into the Promised Land of prosperity but they couldn't believe his awesome power. God's faith is simply acting on what He has told you. And yes, this takes courage especially when your natural senses, the flesh and the devil are barking in your ears to the contrary. But you must take courage and exercise dominion.

When God first gave me the understanding of dominion, I kept hearing in my spirit, "I will make the people "bread" (food) for you." Then, a few days after that, I got several tests in understanding dominion. One particular test the Lord gave me was from a man who I had intended to purchase a used car from for resale. He told me that he would charge me a fee on any car he would purchase for me to resell.

At that time, I didn't have the money to pay the fee. So I had no intention of going to get the car. But the Spirit of God told me to go forward and get the car. When I went to the office the fee was cancelled. God is sovereign; he can make the people into bread! (not literal bread, of course, but the very people who may be your enemy...he can cause them to bless you!)

Many times instead of walking in confidence and dominion, we allow the devil sap our courage. Dominion always has risks and dangers. These can only be surmounted if we "take courage." My brother Dave usually uses this expression when he is trying to comfort and motivate people: "take courage". Taking courage means we face our difficulty with the assurance that God will work it out. True courage is **rage** under the **control** of the Spirit. It's turning off the self-preservation and self-centered modes in our psyche and moving forward with faith and conviction under the inspiration of the Holy Spirit regardless of the costs. This is the only way to bring the abundance of both temporal and spiritual prosperity.

To the newcomer, dominion is reckless abandonment to the Spirit of God.. It's doing crazy things in the Spirit. However, to those who have matured, dominion is walking in faith and love. We have come to love the Father so much that every breath that is drawn is done to please him! Dominion is the essence of life and power in the Spirit, the power that angels flock around and which demons flee.

This is what Jesus strived to teach his "faithless" disciples who constantly cowered in the face of adversity. Their eyes were blinded to the unlimited and irresistible power of God that cannot be withstood. Instead of stepping forward in childlike faith, they allowed their analytical minds to dominate them. But we must free ourselves from this bondage of pride that wants to exalt itself against the knowledge of God and bring every thought into the captivity of Christ. This will bring prosperity in every area of life.

What is prosperity?

We are living in a time where people are being taught that having lots of money is prosperity. Using the scripture, *"Beloved, I wish above all things that thou mayest prosper and be in health, even as they soul prospereth." (John 1:2)*, the doctrine of prosperity has been preached with fervor. This Satanic deception has produced oppressive, insensitive, and prideful Christians. And in many of these circles, poor people are being trampled upon and neglected. Those who are less fortunate are frowned upon as being ignorant and not having any faith.

The truth behind this erroneous teaching is that money usually showcases the deeper spiritual problems that people have in their lives. Whether by financial abundance or lack thereof, money reveals the pride, insecurity, fear, envy, manipulation, pleasure seeking, and jealousy in people's lives. Money to those who do not operate in dominion is seen as security. And when there is plenty or a little, when it comes or doesn't come, it produces strife, confusion, or depression. The flesh floats right to the top. *"For the love of money is the root of all evil; which while some coveted after, thy have erred from the faith, and pierced themselves through with many sorrows." (Timothy 6:16)*

Money always gives a false sense of security and prosperity. Hence, there are those who seek security in a large bank account and investments. But Wall Street can crash overnight. Banks can become insolvent. Money should never be put on a pedestal and worshipped because it is only an instrument of commerce. It is an exchange item to be used for goods and services. That's all money is! It should never become an end in itself. When money is inordinately sought after, it produces covetousness. Covetousness is a greedy and materialistic mindset that grades people by how much they have. This is the mindset that Jesus told people to avoid at all costs. *"Take heed and beware of covetousness: for a man's life consisteth not in the abundance of the things which he posesseth." (Luke 12:15)*

In the Bible, there were many men of God who were affluent. Abraham, Isaac, Job, and Solomon are a few among many who enjoyed God's financial blessing. But note carefully, they did not go after money. God brought the money to them. They obeyed God, then, God in turned gave them wealth. He was the one that gave the wisdom and knowledge to get the money. *"For the Lord giveth riches and added no sorrow."* The Bible teaches plainly that when riches increase one should never set his heart upon it. Men should always use their gifts and talents to get wealth; but wealth should never replace their love for God. Believing that prosperity means an abundance of physical things is a deception. The Bible says, *"But godliness with contentment is great gain. For we brought nothing into this world and it is certain we can carry nothing out. And having food and raiment let us be therewith content." (1 Timothy 6:6-8)*

True prosperity goes beyond investments in the stock market and a home in a prestigious neighborhood; although it may also include this. The essence of true prosperity is contentment. Am I preaching mediocrity? Of course not! Prosperity means that we are walking in complete wholeness in body, soul and spirit. This comes from an intimate relationship with the creator rather that following a few biblical principles and living in a well to-do neighborhood.

Prosperity to a third-world person may be an apartment with adequate space and drinking water nearby. In New York City, prosperity may be a spacious high-rise apartment in an up-scale neighborhood, in Florida a split-level home on an acre with horses. However, in each case it's not the amount of wealth, rather the satisfaction and pleasure in what one has. This is how prosperity must be viewed. The person who is constantly striving for more and more material things is missing the point if they are seeking fulfillment in things. Life's temporary comforts can never give perfect joy and peace, only the Creator can.

We must all seek God's will for our lives and determine his direction for us. He will give us power to get wealth. God has promised faithfully that if we seek his face, He will add the earthly things that we need to us. God wants his people to be prosperous, and prosperity is being contented with God's blessing upon us: whether in little or in much, our faith and obedience to him remains unchanged. This is true prosperity and dominion.

God Plan For Financial Prosperity

"But thou shall remembereth the Lord thy God; for it is He that giveth thee power to get wealth, that he may establish his covenant which he sware unto thy fathers, as it is this day." (Deuteronomy 8:18)

"Honor the Lord with thy substance, and with the first fruits of all thine increase: So shall thy barns be filled with plenty, and thy presses shall burst out with new wine." (Proverbs 2:9-10)

"Will a man rob God? Yet ye have robbed me. But ye say, Wherein have we robbed thee? In tithes and offerings. Ye are cursed with a curse; for ye have robbed me, even this whole nation. Bring ye all the tithes into the storehouse, that there may be meat in mine house,

and prove me now herewith, saith the Lord of host, if I will not open you the windows of heaven, and pour you out a blessing, that there shall not be room enough to receive it. And I will rebuke the devourer for your sakes, and he shall not destroy the fruits of your ground; neither shall our vine cast her fruit before the time in the field, saith the Lord of host. And all nations shall call you blessed; for ye shall be a delightsome land, saith the Lord of host." (Malachi 3:8-12)

"But this I say, He which soweth sparingly shall reap also sparingly; and he which soweth bountifully shall reap also bountifully. Every man according as he purposeth in his heart, so let him give; not grudgingly, or of necessity; for God loveth a cheerful giver. " (2 Corinthians 9:6-7)

"Give and it shall be given unto you good measure, press down and shaken together and running over shall men give unto thy bosom. For with the same measure that ye mete withal it shall be measured to you again." (Luke 6:38)

"He becometh poor that dealeth with a slack hand; but the hand of the diligent maketh rich." (Proverbs 10:4)

"Be thou diligent to know the state of thy flocks, and look well to thy herds." (Proverbs 27:24)

"For wisdom is a defence, and money is a defence: but the excellency of knowledge is, that wisdom giveth life to them that have it." (Ecclesiastes 7:12)

"Much food is in the tillage of the poor; but there is that is destroyed for want of judgment." (Proverbs 14:23)

"He that loveth pleasure shall be a poor man: he that loveth wine and oil shall not be rich." (Proverbs 21:17)

"He also that is slothful in his work is brother to him that is a great waster." (Proverbs 18:9)

As long as we are upon this earth, we must remember that money is our means of upkeep. The wise man Solomon puts it this way, *"A feast is made for laughter, and wine maketh merry: but **money answereth all things**." (Ecclesiastes 10:19)* So, when God puts money in our hand, we need to know what to do. Herein lies the way to prosperity, contentment, and dominion. Firstly, when God gives money he expects us to honor and recognize the person who gave it. This is called tithing and giving. We should take a tenth of our income and deposit it in the house of God, along with other monetary gifts. Then we must pay those who we owe because of services and goods we have purchased: light, water, telephone, grocery, etc. Then, we should consider those who are in need. Then comes savings, investment and pleasure!

Giving is a fundamental teaching of the kingdom of God that we can never circumvent. It is a sign of love and self-sacrifice when it is done out of obedience and compassion. When a person is operating in dominion they can give their last and still feel good. They can give to those in need and not think they were "had." Money is not the issue, God's will is. When we are shackled by our fleshly thinking, we are always looking out for number one. We are overly concerned about our own needs. Dominion gives us the freedom and confidence to look beyond the few dollars that we give to God who is able to supply all our needs.

When we give we can expect God to give back to us according to his word. It may not come the day after we have put fifty dollars in the offering or after our tithes envelope was collected but it will come.

God's timing is different from ours. While we are looking through imperfect faith and a dark glass, God in His sovereignty knows exactly when to let the blessing flow. Many people become frustrated when God doesn't show up when they expect him. However, I am learning to relax, let go, and let God. Prosperity will come!

While operating in dominion, we must always be open to the voice of God and be flexible when he wants us to change the routine a little. For example, I had just taken my tithe money from my bank account to carry to church on Sunday. I was walking out to lunch, when I met a Christian brother who I had not seen for almost a year. The Holy Spirit said, "Give him fifty dollars." Some people would have immediately started rebuking the devil. But what was more important, a brother in desperate need, or carrying the tithe to church on Sunday? Yes, God wants us to be obedient in our tithing but I am sure He is much more concerned about the brother in desperate need. One need was more urgent that the other. This is dominion; flowing in the Spirit of God! A year later, that same brother related to me how God had really met his need that day.

But while we operate in dominion we must guard against passivity. When a man exhibits passivity in financial management, the Devil can wreak havoc on a marriage and family. The Bible says, *"A feast is made for laughter, and wine maketh merry; but money answereth all things." (Ecclesiastes 10:19)* Many marriages have been dissolved because of poor financial management and debt burden. With proper financial management in place, the family can be spared much anguish, frustration and embarrassment. Also, when a man exercises sound financial management, it shows good leadership skills that will gain the respect of his wife.

But who should handle the money? How much money should be spent without advising your spouse? What about debt servicing and purchasing of assets? Time and time again, I hear men say that they are not proficient in the area of financial management or some other area and have turned this area over to their wives. Whereas, a man should welcome his wife's advice, talents and assistance, he can not give up the responsibility of overseer and leader. If he does, it's a sure sign of slothfulness and ignorance in leadership. Remember, a good leader never does all the work and must delegate tasks to others. So, if your wife is proficient in finances, you are a blessed man, let her help you. Give her the opportunity to budget in consultation with you; however, continue to be alert and watchful as a good steward over the blessing that God has given him.

Sit down with your wife to discuss and come to agreement with regard to spending of the family's income. This is the sign of a good leader who recognizes that he cannot do it alone. The husband and the wife are designed to operate as one unit. Listen to you wife's advice and implement those things you know will benefit the family. This will serve to eliminate strife and insecurity that sometimes arise, when one spouse is unaware of what the other spouse is doing with the money.

When you have done this, learn to dominate money, this is the key to financial prosperity. Never allow money to dominate you. Develop habits of budgeting and thriftiness. Develop habits of maximizing income and minimizing expenses. Listen to the Spirit of God as he gives wisdom and direction while shopping or spending. Pay attention to household expenses to ensure conservation and prudence.

Try to conserve as must as possible, but don't be a prig or slave driver about it. Being critical and overbearing will ostracize your family. Rather, use the gentle but firm approach coupled with love. If you are in your spiritual position, the Holy Spirit will help motivate family members. Just do you part of encouragement to conserve.

A good way to conserve is by learning to do some repairs and maintenance work yourself. God can give you wisdom to be a handyman! This can cut down enormously on the household budget. For example, the house needs painting or the car may need a tune-up. Don't wait until the walls of your home become an eyesore before you react or the car stalls on a major highway. Be proactive instead of reactionary, look for wear and tear and fix and maintain as needed. The Bible says, that the way of the slothful is as a hedge of thorns but the way of the just is plain. In this scripture, laziness is polarized with being righteous. Laziness is rebellion against God mandate for fervency in business.

Freedom From Self the Way to Excellence

"The sluggard is wiser in his own conceit that seven men that can render a reason." (Proverbs 26:16)

"He also that is slothful in his work is brother to him that is a great waster." (Proverbs 18:9)

As long as we are in love with ourselves, we will never let go and let God. God wants so much to endure us with supernatural wisdom and energize us with His power, so that we could confront challenges instead of running from them. He wants to flow through us like a river, but we cling to the old wineskin and old garments instead of letting go and letting God. Divine wisdom is available for all men. All we have to do is ask, *"If any of you lack wisdom, let him ask of God, that giveth to all men liberally, and upbraideth not; and it shall be given him. But let him ask in faith nothing wavering. For he that wavereth is like a wave of the sea driven with the wind and tossed." (James 1:5-6)*

Usually when we see lethargy in men, we assume that it is a discipline problem. In a superficial way, lack of discipline may have played a part in this behavior. However, behind this slothfulness lies a spirit of negative pride; a stubborn and fearful spirit that avoid problems and work instead of accepting and working through challenges. The cure for negative pride is not the school of discipline as most think. The school of discipline may help, but it will still leave the cancer of negative pride intact. Pride has to be broken through humility and genuine repentance. This is God's way to bring a man to a higher level of discipline where he can confront challenges and work through them.

I think if anyone has struggled with dominion, it's me. It seemed that every time, I came that close to defeating debt and bringing prosperity to my family, the enemy would step in and create havoc financially. Then instead of listening to my wife's tender rebuke and advice, I would continue the endless cycle of borrowing. I just had to do it just one more time. Ah! If I could just do it over again! But God knows all things and these experiences can benefit another man who is determined not to walk the halls of mediocrity, when everything is available to him.

My problem was not that I spent too much or was pleasure centered, although some of this may have contributed to my dilemma. My problem was patience. Patience to sit back, relax, and enjoy the ride. I simply refused to let God take the lead. My opinion, my fears, and insecurity usually drowned out the voice of God, making me susceptible to Satan's lies. Like an adulterous woman, I was making love to two men. I wanted God to lead, I prayed that he would lead me but I always depended on my own human reasoning.

But our God wants us to move forward in pure and absolute faith. This means listening only to His voice. Yes, he wants our debts repaid, our family in order and our children saved. But we retreat too often in fear and insecurity. I am here to encourage you, man of God, that you are more than a conqueror. The victory has already been won. All God wants you to do is distribute the spoils. The devil constantly puts up mirages before us. "It's not going to work out. You'll be a fool to listen to that. People have been trying that faith business for years and they haven't succeeded." Don't listen to him! Faith is your victory!!! God is our Father and he will never let us down. The Bible says to us that we should let God be true and every man a liar and God has said, *"Behold, I give unto you power to tread on serpents and scorpions, and over all the power of the enemy and nothing shall by any means hurt you." (Luke 10:10)*

Part Three

Understanding Her Feminine Side

Introduction

There is something about the divine makeup of a woman that is awesomely therapeutic. It begins with the gentle touch of her hand soothing her hurting child, to the tender touch of her fingers caressing the tiny nerves that race back and forth through her husband's body. We can also see it in the creativity of her hands as it beautifies her home. Birthed in the very depth of her heart and spirit, these qualities reveal her feminine side.

This nurturing side of womanhood is an essential part of her divine makeup and provides an avenue for her to soothe the hearts and souls of those around her. From the physical love of her husband to the emotional needs of her children, she has been divinely empowered to help her family to their next level of maturity. Indeed, she is the iron that sharpens iron.

I often think about how Satan used the feminine nature to snatch away dominion from mankind. Satan used the woman to fulfill his devious plan of domination and control. However, this need not be a reason for shame or disgrace. God has already empowered us, as women, to snatch dominion back from the devil. By his grace, we will walk in our divine purposes, we will be obedient to His word, and we will overcome the struggles of the flesh. My sister, the sun is shining brightly and it's time to blossom. Yes, it's time to be all that God called you to be. And it can happen if we embrace our feminine side!!

But speak thou the things that becometh sound doctrine.......
the aged women likewise, that they be in behavior as becometh holiness,
not false accusers, not given to much wine, teachers of good
things; that they may teach the young women to be sober, to love their husbands, to love their children, to be discreet,
chaste, keepers at home,
good, obedient to
their own
husbands,
to love
their
children.
(Titus 2:3-5)

9. I Love My Husband!

I still smile when I think about the first time I saw my husband. He was the tall, slim young man in the front row of our Church's annual convention, lifting his hands as he sang during a worship service. For a minute, I wondered why he wasn't outside with most of the other young men trying to catch the attention of the ladies. Then he did something that really got my attention, he fell on his knees in worship. In the small island community where I grew up, this was not common. At that moment, I knew that there was something different about him.

I didn't see him again for several months until I met him later at a bible training institute. He was late getting to class that night, and the only vacant seat was directly in front of me. I said silently, "Good work, Jesus!" I was bought up to believe that a woman was not to assert herself with a man, so I waited for this young man to make a move and take the lead. He did! A few nights later, just before a class break, we spoke to each other for the first time! It wasn't long before he began talking to me, but it didn't end there.

Three weeks later he asked me to marry him. "Yes," I said, "I would love to be your wife." I invited him to dinner the following Sunday to meet my family, and eighteen months later, we were married. I knew God had given me a gem and I vowed to love, honor, and obey him, but I was still in fantasy land. It wasn't long before I realized that my prince charming was not faultless. Nonetheless, I had made a covenant and a commitment to stand by him, come rain or shine, and love him for as long as we both lived. That was more than twenty-two years ago and today, I still love my husband!

> *"The aged women likewise, that they be in behavior as becometh holiness, not false accusers, not given to much wine, teachers of good things; That they may teach the young women to be sober, to love their husbands, to love their children, To be discreet, chaste, keepers at home,*

> good, obedient to their own husbands, that the word of God be not blasphemed." (Titus 2:3-5)

> "Nevertheless let every one of you in particular so love his wife even as himself; and the wife see that she reverence her husband." (Ephesians 5: 33)

God's mandate to every woman is to reverence and love her husband. Some might say, "...but you don't know the man I married, he is a womanizer, a cheat, or a pathetic drunk." Or, maybe he's selfish, mean, or controlling. However, regardless of the type of person your husband is, God's mandate doesn't change. I know it's easy to think that the women who love their husbands are those whose husbands are sweet, kind, and doing everything right. But remember, there is not one perfect man on the face of the earth. They all come with faults and failures. In most cases, you have to choose which faults or failures you prefer to live with.

Most women select the men in their lives according to how he will make her look. If he is handsome, then she believes everyone would admire her handsome husband or her beautiful babies. Others look for someone who is educated or financially secure, so that he can give her the life she desires. Still, there are those who look for the man from an influential family, so that she can live in the lime-light. Few women choose a man because of who he really is in character and spirit. As a result, they usually reap the results of their misguided decisions. However, even if our husbands are not all that they are supposed to be, we can still be all that we can be.   In the book of Titus chapter two, the responsibility rested in the hands of older, or spiritually mature women to teach the young women how to lead godly lives, love their husbands, and serve their families.

Most women have no problem serving their children, but they think twice when told to serve their husbands. In the era that we live in, the thought of embracing a submissive attitude is considered subservient, or outdated. A meek and quiet woman is ancient history, and born is the independent and multifaceted career-oriented feminine success. Without realizing it, we have become more selfish and self-centered. And, how has this affected us? Divorce rates have escalated as husbands and wives have grown apart. Children are forced to grow up unattended and without the nurture of mother. Communities struggle with the high crime rates as a direct result of bitterness and anger that stem from broken homes.

God created the man and woman to work together as a team. An independent spirit fights unity and service to husband and family. It desires control rather than humble submission. It seeks its own way rather than the ways of the Lord. Ultimately, it seeks to dispose of the husband's rightful place as head of the home. Instead of supporting him, the independent spirit seeks to undermine his every decision.

The devil has devised an all-out attack against our husbands, and many wives have joined in to help clobber them. Husbands in today's homes have almost no respect or significance and many are treated like the hired servants. And like us, with a misunderstanding of their true role in the home, they usually make matters worse. Few, understand who they are and the awesome responsibility that they carry.

My husband Lambert did not grow up with his birth father in the home, but after he gave his life to Christ in his later teen years, God provided strong Christian men in the church who stood by him and instructed him according to the bible. There was one older gentleman by the name of Fred, that he enjoyed visiting with when he began attending one of the local churches. Bishop Fred, an eighty-three year old man would often give Lambert advice. Once, he told Lambert, "Do not run around from girl to girl in the church, but ask God to send you a wife and settle yourself down."

And that's what he did! One of the things that drew me to Lambert was his obvious commitment to Christ. I had been praying that God would give me a husband that loved me with all his heart, but loved the Lord even more. My reasoning was that if he truly loved the Lord, then he would want to walk according to His word. If he did what the bible said concerning his home and family, then I would be okay.

God answered my prayer! I loved the man that God gave me and because I loved him, I desired to honor him as head of our home. I wanted him to be all that God had ordained him to be. I enjoyed serving him, caring for him, encouraging and praying for him often. But, I was young, and many times I faltered. There were times I purposely disobey him. There were times I argued to get my way and the lists goes on.

At those times, I didn't realize how crucial and valuable my role was to the success of my husband and family. Like most woman of our time, instead of building him up, I was breaking him down. With our many accomplishments and rights, we believe the lie that we don't really need a man in our lives, or worse that we are not a vital part of his destiny.

Without teamwork and unity a relationship will become one-sided and ineffective. **We need to work with our husbands recognizing and honoring them as the earthly leaders in the home.** And, as always, a strong leader is an asset to any company. In fact, without a strong and courageous leader companies and organizations usually do poorly. When a leader is not strong, he makes poor decisions; they procrastinate and become passive because they are afraid of responsibility or making mistakes.

That's why it's important for a woman to always speak positively to her husband. Destroy the leader and you destroy yourself. When the head rolls away the rest of the body is left handicapped. Your encouragement goes a long way in strengthening and supporting your husband. It motivates him as he makes decisions from a position of security, knowing that he has his wife's support.

Love is a very powerful tool. It builds, it nourishes, it corrects, and it heals. It is more than the utterance of words, but it is a display of the heart. It is easy to say, "I love you, honey!" But what about when that man has a problem or fault, are we willing to work with him? Is his wife committed to praying for him until God brings deliverance? Will she stand beside him in the glad times as well as the hard times?

Contrary to popular belief, marriage is a step of faith.. When we commit ourselves to a relationship of this magnitude, we must be willing to hang in there for better or worse. True love will not give in at the first sign of trouble. It will not report him to the in-laws. True love will seek ways and means to help a spouse stand on his feet again. It will offer kind words and not walk away in disgust; this is what we must aim for.

The woman that adores her husband has an earnest desire to please him. Love that is alive, looks for every opportunity to express itself. The joy of lovemaking in a marriage is the ultimate physical expression of love. It's the icing on the cake of a developing marriage. Lovemaking is more than kissing and cuddling. It is helping your man to relax and forget about the pressures that come with every-day life. It is nurturing and soothing his spirit so that he is energized to walk out and conquer the challenges of each day.

Love was intended to be so beautiful when shared by two people. It is empowering, fulfilling, and very binding. Anyone can have a sexual relationship simply for the purpose physical gratification, but in a marriage relationship the purpose changes. It becomes a total surrendering of self, a divine act of unselfishness. The woman who loves her husband values the opportunity to prepare a comfortable place for him to lay his head. Whether it is on her breast or his easy chair she wants to make sure that he is contented.

Pleasure comes wrapped up in many packages. It can be as simple as being a true friend or as deep as the passion in our souls. Whichever one a wife has to serve up, she gives with everything that she has. Many people do not look favorably on marital love because it appears to be unreal and superficial. There are individuals in this day and age who are intimidated at the thought of a relationship with one partner for a lifetime.

Many people today want to jump in and out of relationships looking for that one perfect lover. Nevertheless, what is marriage without the promise of commitment? It seems everywhere we look we see love being advertised, but it is a love that is based primarily on feelings. However, feelings come and go. For this reason, love must go beyond feeling to faith. Work with what you have! Understand that even when you do not feel it, it is still there. Sometimes it just needs to be stimulated, watered, or released, but it is there!

Love matures in time. When I think back to the days of our courtship, I can honestly say that the love I have toward my husband today far exceeds what I felt then. In fact, I love him more today than I loved him just a few years ago. It seems the longer we are together, and the more we endure together, the stronger our bond becomes. There are times when I might be angry over a matter and 'feel' as though the love has gone to sleep, but very quickly these 'feelings or misgivings' evaporate and commitment comes in to bridge the gap until love is awakened again. Love is also respect. The way you talk to him, refer to him, and walk beside him is a demonstration of the love that is in your heart.

The essence of loving is giving, and this becomes the depth of your marriage relationship. Jesus proved this to us when he came in human flesh to show us how to esteem others more highly than ourselves. We are encouraged to give without asking anything in return. The depth of our relationship with him, and our ability to love and honor him, is revealed when we love and honor our fellow human beings. Jesus admonished his disciples saying, "This is my commandment, that ye love one another, as I have loved you. Greater love hath no man than this, that a man lay down his life for his friends (John 15:12-13). This is the challenge: to love like Jesus loved.

It is expected of those of us that say we are Christians to not only work for Christ, but to love the Lord with all our heart, and our neighbor (those you live around each day) as yourself. Aim to focus on what you can do for your husband, and not what he can do for you. Ask God daily for wisdom to be the wife that your husband needs. Do not allow others to point out the faults that he might have, but lift him up to God who alone knows the intent of every man's heart. Woman, know that you have been divinely equipped with what your husband needs. If you allow God to use you, he will take the weakest link and make it strong and powerful with each passing day.

10. Welcome to Motherhood

I have always felt that there was something very special about the role of a mother. When I was a little girl, I would watch my mom around our home, and she just seemed to make everything come to life. When she moved the furniture around, the room would look more inviting and cozy.

She was always busy making sure that everything in the house was in order and as they said it in the old days, "spick-n-span." It was a real treat and pleasure to come home to an environment like that; inviting, peaceful and clean.

In 1995, after the death of my infant daughter Kymille, I decided to become a homemaker. I released my full-time housekeeper, walked away from the workplace, and went home for good. I had wrestled with the idea for a few years, but when this tragedy occurred, I realized at that time that this was the best decision for our family. It was a struggle at first and there were moments when I thought of maybe going back to work at least part time. But, after a few weeks, my husband and children were convinced that mommy's place was at home.

I believe that a lot of women would prefer to stay at home with their children but aren't able to because of financial or other constraints. However, I believe that God will make a way, if we step out in true faith and obedience to His word. I believe that he will give us the wisdom to stretch our finances like the woman in Proverbs 31. But, we must have a determined desire and know that it is God's will and timing.

In Genesis chapter one, God gave a charge to the woman and man to be fruitful and multiply. Some people take this to mean childbearing. However, to be fruitful and to multiply means more than bringing forth children physically. As mothers, we must learn to empower our children spiritually, emotionally, and socially.

Many mothers in our present society do not have time for mothering because of busy schedules. There are also women today who consider having children a distraction and an impediment to having a successful career. To them, the challenges of rearing children are an unnecessary burden.

However, to those women who want to embrace motherhood, your greatest asset is your godly seed; Godly seed that can make a difference in a very ungodly world. A mother is one of the greatest forces of influence in the lives of her children. When we think of the way she carries her babies within her body, and pushes them through the birth canal, she is positioned as their gateway to the world.

She has the opportunity to pour into her children all the wisdom that she has within herself. Her life becomes an example of grace and humility from which her children can receive and learn. Her nurturing and devotion become a major source of strength for her offspring. They will then move forth from birth and to empower others as they mature. It is for this reason that we as mothers must make every effort to do all that we can to positively empower the lives of our children.

Satan, the deceiver, is aware of the potential of the woman's seed, and he fights tooth and nail for the lives of children. One of his schemes is to distract the young mother during the most impressionable years of her child's life. It is often at this time that he creeps in to wound or damage a child's spirit. There are mothers who painfully look back over their youthful days, and realize that when their children needed them most, they were unable to be there. The girl who was molested because mother was at work, the little boy who spent his growing years in front of violent video games, the child that was brought up by the nanny are examples of neglected motherhood.

One of a child's primary needs is the dedicated and attentive love of its mother. Without the proper guidance of parents, children will easily be lead astray. They have not been properly trained to handle relationships, and thus, they are easy prey for manipulators and predators.

Also, in these early years, there is always the possibility for seeds of resentment, bitterness, and anger to grow if proper nurturing through communication is not done. When our children experience rejection from friends, teachers, or even family members, it is important to be an avenue where they can release their frustrations in an atmosphere of unconditional love. This is the essence of motherhood. You are loved no matter what.

We must encourage our young women to treasure the calling of motherhood. Married, widowed, or single mothers today must understand the awesome responsibility that they have to God for the rearing of children and training of the young. Too often careers and dreams are seen as the most important accomplishments in a young woman's life. While these things are desirable in their place, they can never bring the fulfillment of motherhood.

My first experience with motherhood came about eighteen months after I was married. I gave birth to Lambert Jr. about 6 a.m. in the morning. I had always longed for the day when I would have a child of my own, and as the doctor placed him in my arms, there was a sense of fear and joy. Fear of enormity of the responsibility of having this little life dependent upon me, but joy in knowing that God had given us this little miracle. Later that night after the nurses had left us alone, I lifted him up to the Lord, and asked for wisdom and direction in meeting the needs of this child, the first of four angels. I needed the help of God to train him up so that he could become a vessel worthy for the master's use. As the days turned to months, and the months turned into years, I came to understand that being a mother is more than a heart's desire, it is a place of immense responsibility.

I was in the city of Jacksonville, Florida for a speaking engagement, when I spotted the headline in the morning paper. The faces of two men and two women were pasted across the page under the caption, "Do you know who is watching your children?" The newspaper article exposed the arrest of the four, accused of physically and sexually abusing local children in a daycare center. This shocking discovery alone shows the urgent need for mothers to return to full time care of their children. More and more mothers are coming to the realization that they are indeed the most important mentors in the lives of their children. It is a fact that, in order to sufficiently affect their lives, parents must become very dependent on God and his Word.

In these days in which we live, evil is on the rampage to snuff out the innocence of our children. Never before has it been more urgent for parents to make an investment into the training and nurturing of their offspring. There is no amount of material gain that can be compared to the visible presence of a mother. Like everything else in life, motherhood requires time. I look at each of my children and understand that each one is different, and requires something different from me. I must find time for all of them both collectively and individually. It never ceases to amaze me how much they desire their own private moments with me, and how getting it affects them. My youngest daughter might request that I join her in a game, or some other activity. My older daughter prefers outings, while my son enjoys being loved on and relaxing with quiet talks. As they mature, their needs will change and so must I.

A woman needs time, not only for nurturing, but also for preparing herself to minister and to care for her family as a whole. The ministry of motherhood is intended to be a full-time position. It demands tenacity, submission, patience and a profound faith in God. A woman needs personal time to prepare her spirit, and quiet moments to rest in the presence of the Lord. This helps to keep her spirit pure. This time of devotion and prayer is also known as intercession. Intercession is formed from the word "intercede" which comes from the root word "inter" which means "between" and "cede" which means to go. This means a mother must sometimes act as a "go between" for children by interceding on their behalf. With the woman being a natural intercessor, she can intercede for herself, her family, and her community.

When a mother loves her children with a kind and committed heart, they become as beautiful as she is. Somehow, I always felt motherhood came naturally to women until I met Joanne (not her real name). I received her call late one evening. "I just need someone to talk to," she said, "before I take my life." She went on to say how situations in her life and home were getting worse, and she felt as if she could not take anymore. I could hear the voices of her children in the background, and we talked a while about how her decision would affect them. She replied, "It's for the best, I have nothing to offer them, and besides they will get over it, after all I did."

At that moment, I realized that she was dealing with deep dark wounds. As I prayed for the leading of the Holy Spirit to minister to her conscience, her life story came pouring out. She grew up never knowing her father, in a home that was cold and unloving. Rejection and neglect had become permanent fixtures. She knew them well. As she grew she was forced to sell her body to various men who passed through her home. Her wounded heart mistook this for love. She constantly heard her mother say to her and her siblings, "I hate you! "You've messed up my life!" Soon Joanne came to believe these words.

As the middle of three children, she craved attention, careful of every opportunity to do anything or go anywhere just to be accepted. She said to me, "All I wanted was for my mother to love me like she loved those men." Soon, like her mother, she began searching for love in the arms of men. She eventually married but the marriage was full of tension, bickering and infidelity. Finally, after much frustration, fighting, marital unfaithfulness, and regrets, her husband took the children and walked out. Joanne was devastated, and her every moment was spent trying to win him back.

But, even after her family returned, Joanne was not happy and would often abuse them verbally. She realized that she was wounding her children just as her mom had wounded her. This troubled her, as she tried to understand why she never felt the motherly feelings other mothers spoke about. There was never that bonding with her children. She did not know how to love them, or anyone else for that matter, and now she just wanted to die. That night Joanne received a breakthrough. Over a period of time, tears, and ministering of the word, she was able to stand on her feet again. The last time I saw her, she was with her husband and they had made a commitment to rebuilding their lives and family.

Many women find themselves in this predicament. They lack a proper foundation. No one showed them how to love, or care for their families. It is the ministry of womanhood that teaches the younger women how to be mothers.

Like Joanne, many young women do not have the privilege of a godly example. We live in a time when it is not deemed necessary for a woman to just stay home, or spend the time that is needed to foster and prepare children for the times before them. We are still faced today with all the good and evil that existed from the beginning of time. In order to combat it, we need faith in God and submission to his word. Children still need care. Homes must still be provided for, and fathers must still till the ground as wives continue to be a helpmeet for their husbands. All of these facets need to be in place for the systems to flow in the home. A lack of any one of these could cause a disaster.

God continues to strive with all of us, desiring to show us how to live amidst the deception of the enemy. However, in a fallen state, we continue to resist and fail. Our lives are at stake and so are the lives of our children. When we reject God's plan, unwittingly we embrace the Devil's plan. This reminds me of a former schoolmate of mine who after having her first child desired to raise her as a full time mom. At the time both, she and her husband held good jobs, and did not see how they could live on one salary, but they prayed for guidance. Amidst criticism, they decided to make the sacrifice and stepped out in faith.

As her child grew older, Angela (not her real name) started a small home business to assist her husband with the financial needs of the family. Things were difficult, and many encouraged her to go back to work, but she refused to place her child in daycare. Within a few years, God blessed the business so much that the profits fully supported the family. Today, she is happy and financially stable. When we are obedient to God, blessings will flow. Many look at the obstacles and challenges, and become fearful, but when we trust in the Lord, and allow him to direct our path, we will eventually reap the harvest.

As women desirous of the will of the Lord in our lives, we must take a stand to do all that God has called us to do, and be. I know that this is a very controversial time and topic, but it is crucial to our families that we be faithful to the word of God. Situations beyond their control cause many women to have to leave their children and go out of the home in order to provide for the family. There are single and widowed women with children, or a woman whose husband may be disabled, and she may have to support the home temporarily. Yet, even in these cases, God is able to grant the desires of the heart. God is able to remove that which can hinder, to enable us to walk according to His Divine Will.

There are also women who want to be home with their children as well as fulfill dreams of acquiring assets through business and investments. This does not mean that they cannot seek to realize these dreams. God has blessed women with creative talents and abilities and he intends for them to use every one. With the level of technology that exists today, it is becoming more convenient for parents to establish home businesses and work from home. It can become very beneficial for a mother with school-aged children, in that she is able to be at home for her children and at the same time assist her husband financially while using her God-given talents.

Having the opportunity to fulfill her dreams can be emotionally rewarding. Women like Martha Stewart capitalized on God-given talents that have greatly aided her and many other women in expressing themselves at home. What is important in the midst of our pursuits is taking steps to ensure that we are not distracted from the central or ultimate focus, which is our family. We must be careful not to allow external distractions to consume too much of our time and attention. Pray and ask the Lord for wisdom before any move or major decision. I would encourage young women to further their education, and enter into the job market at will. However, when we choose to be married and bear children, we must be prepared to sacrifice our needs and wants for the betterment of our family. When one accepts the responsibility of marriage and then motherhood, the external must take second place behind what is most important for her husband and children.

Some wives face the challenge of a husband who will not hear of his wife being a homemaker. This situation can be frustrating and disappointing. It will bring division in the marriage relationship, like all other conflicts. Even though it is the will of God for the woman to stay at home, this woman must respect the position of her husband, and entrust the situation to God, allowing him to work it out for her. There are times when victory may be immediate, other times we must patiently wait on God. I encourage mothers to train their sons for the responsibility of headship that lies before them. Helping them as much as possible to prepare to lead and take care of their home and family.

In a marriage, there may be areas in both your lives that God is working out. The important thing is that your desires are in accordance with God's word. Our prayer must be, "Lord, give me the wisdom in making decisions according to your will for my life." Do not take this position lightly if we desire to reap godly results. Just as important as the physical mother, is the spiritual mother or shepherd. Many young women may not have a mother who can minister to them, but God has placed in the body women who are equipped to minister to their biological children, as well as others. As with adoption or foster care, children are at times placed into the hands of guardians who will love and instruct them in the ways of the Lord. In our spiritual lives, there is also a need for guidance from those that are mature in the things of God. Their shepherding, or spiritual mothering, holds the weaker one steady until he or she is able to walk on his or her own. The lives that God has placed into our hands will continue to change generations. When you offer a child your hand it may last but for a moment, but when you offer your heart, it will last a lifetime.

11. Keeper of the Home

You can experience a therapeutic moment when you walk into a home that is fresh, clean, and well decorated; and most of all, a place where you can sense peace and tranquility. Many new home developers open the doors to model homes to give home buyers a taste of what can become their own. They decorate these houses with vibrant, beautiful colors that compliment the tasteful furnishings and floor coverings. The atmosphere is set with soft music and the scent of freshly baked cookies to evoke a feeling of nostalgia and longing in the heart of prospective home buyers. I am convinced that every home can resemble a model; all that is needed is a homemaker.

Home is the place we long for, the place we feel most relaxed, where the family runs to, and a woman can bask in. Her loving heart in the home nurtures the spirit of those who enter, dispersing warmth, happiness and peacefulness. Those who enter feel welcomed and look forward to returning.

Many homes today are in shambles because they lack a homemaker. Because the homemaker is the one who maintains the home, and keep things in order, it is a major hazard to run any home without her. Even model homes, though empty of occupants, must be cared for on a daily basis. Can you imagine a city without policemen or concerned residents? The thieves would settle in, crime will build up, and very soon that area of town would be in ruins. Well, the same is true of a home without a good housekeeper. The dirt will settle in, the dust will build up, and that home will become a mess.

The position of a homemaker is more than a career; it is a means of survival for every home. Like every other career choice, the woman who chooses to be a homemaker must give both time and commitment to ensure daily success. The more time and devotion she puts into it, the better the results.

But, what does it really mean to be a keeper at home? This very vital position is demonstrated in Proverbs 31, which focuses on a model wife and mother. There was a time when I envied the proverb 31 woman, until I realized that she is a standard for women to follow. She was a woman of great patience, emanating virtue and faith. She was dedicated to the upkeep of her home, the rearing of her children, while under girding her husband and supervising her workers.

Traditionally, women in that day and time were deeply committed to maintaining and establishing their homes. The normal duties of these women were drawing water, grinding grain, spinning wool, weaving fabric, sewing clothing, laundering garments, preparing meals, and taking care of the needs of their husband and children. Social responsibilities included hosting travelers, and guests with food and rest.

Spiritual responsibilities found mothers shaping spiritual values in their children, preparing their families for worship, and taking them to the temple. These routine tasks were a woman's top priority. We can see these things manifested in the lives of women like Dorcas, Lydia, and the Proverbs 31 woman. The virtuous woman did all this and more. She went beyond the call of duty. Her industrious and creative heart was centered on her family and household. So blessed was her family that they rose up with grateful appreciation, because of her commitment. The principles practiced within her home also aided her economically. It began within her heart, took root in her home, and finally extended to the outside world.

There is an urgent need in our communities today for committed homemakers. The home is like a manufacturing plant that sets a course for every member of the family. Sadly, the average woman today spends less than a third of each day attending to the needs of her family and home. Most of her time is filled with other commitments that make it very difficult for her to meet the vital needs of her family.

On an average, most women get between 6-8 hours of sleep. Another eight hours are allocated to work or career, not to mention the time that is spent commuting to and from work. When she finally arrives back in her home, it is now early evening; however her real work has just begun. She has to cook, clean up, and do laundry or other household chores. In most cases, tidying up her house has to wait because she is tired, or something else has taken priority over that chore.

She might have an hour to help kids with homework or sort through mail, before retiring to a bed that she did not have time to make up that morning.

It is now late in the evening, and she begins to prepare for the next day. But first she has to put the kids to bed, or maybe entertain an occasional friend or neighbor. If she has extra commitments such as church activities, study classes, or civil organizations, PTA etc, these is take from the hours in the evening or sleep time. When she finally falls next to her husband, intimacy is the last wish on her list. If this pattern continues, her marriage could eventually wither and die.

Even when it appears everything is well, the working woman knows her life can very easily spin out of control. Having a full time career may be necessary and self-satisfying, but it carries a very expensive price tag for any family. The weight of this price tag can be seen in statistical reports that are reflective of current home life. The book of Proverbs tells us that, *"The rod and reproof give wisdom, but a child left to himself bringeth his mother to shame, (Proverb 29:15).* How many children are left alone because parents are not able to offer the kind of attention and instruction that they need? It doesn't end there, how many marriages are destroyed by the added stress in the home, caused by external pressure, and the dilemmas of a home neglected? Indeed, the very foundation of our nation is shaken because of neglect and rejection in so many crucial areas of our lives. I would like to share a letter that I received from a young woman whose personal experience is indicative of this conclusion.

Dear Kim,

I grew up in a very sheltered home. We were not millionaires, but we never seemed to lack anything. My mom and dad worked in very influential positions and so as a very little girl, I was always used to having a housekeeper around our home. When I got up in the morning, I left my room a mess, but when I got home it was always clean, and food was cooked, I never got involved. As most young women do, I desired to get married and I did. My husband and I went on a beautiful honeymoon, given to us by my parents as a wedding gift. It seemed everything was perfect until we came back home to live as husband and wife.

I will never forget our first meal. I wanted to cook something simple, but the meal though simple was a disaster. My new husband said to me "that's alright honey, lets go to my mother's for something or we can eat out, things will get better." The trouble is it never got better. The truth was that I didn't know how to cook. In my home, I had never learned to cook, clean, iron, or anything else, like most young girls did. My mom never told me it was important for me to learn these things. I responded to my husband pretty much the way my mom responded to hers, and it drove a wedge between us.

I had graduated from college with honors and got a well paying job that I was good at. I moved up the ladder of success quickly, but when I got married I found that none of these things prepared me for marriage. My husband soon began to go by his parent's home quite often to get our dinner and to relax. He said it was hard to relax in a dirty house. Eventually, I did what I thought was best, I got a housekeeper. Then things really began to fall apart when I felt the young housekeeper was becoming attracted to my husband. I had to act quickly, fearing I'd lose my marriage, so I fired her. For a while, I really tried to commit to keeping things in order, but I couldn't.

After a few weeks I decided to hire another housekeeper, but one that was much older. The lady that came into our life was not just a helper, she was an angel. She not only kept my house, but she taught me how to cook, clean, bake, care for my husband, and fight for my marriage. This Christian woman poured herself into me, and showed me what it was to be a godly woman. My good looks didn't do it, nor an active sex life. It was the power of God working through this woman to teach me what I desperately needed to know.

Your article in the last issue of your magazine where you stressed the importance of training our children in the right way really hit home. It brought tears to my eyes as I thought of how close I came to losing my marriage. Mothers today must be encouraged to teach their children the ways of the word. Too many young girls are going down the aisle with one thing on their mind- sex. Like me, they don't know how to cook, clean, keep house, or keep a husband. In many homes, parents are pre-occupied with building careers, going to school, working overtime, or rediscovering their youth, to teach their children how to be responsible adults. We say the divorce rate is climbing. Here lies the major problem. We are running after the wrong things, and we are not giving our children the right examples to follow. Daddy is never home, and fails to take care of the family, so the sons grow up to do the same thing. Mom comes home too late to cook or clean, the house is filthy and food is ordered out. When our daughters get married, they continue what they have learned.

My parents were good moral people, but they were not Christians, so they were unable to impart God's word to their children. As a result, I was never interested in Christianity in my youth, but it is amazing how God reaches us through the dark times in our lives, when things take a turn for the worst. I thank God I acted quickly, or I too might have been another statistic. Today I have two sons and a daughter, whom my husband and I are teaching responsibility, accountability, honesty, and godliness. I will not allow my children to grow up as I did. As a homemaker I have made some major sacrifices, but they are worth it. My husband is now a Christian and our marriage continues to grow from strength to strength. To God Be the GLORY!

> *The price of neglect and absence*
> *Is but a down payment,*
> *There's no way of knowing the cost,*
> *For money can't conquer the hearts that are broken,*
> *Nor buy back the souls that are lost.*

There was a time in my life when I felt I could do it all: the duties of a wife, mother, the homemaking, and balance a career at the same time. Finally, I realized that the world of super woman was a fantasy. I found myself struggling to get it all done properly, and as a result my family suffered, as well as myself. Many evenings I came home so exhausted that I was too tired to enjoy my children when they came running to mommy just to get a hug or some attention.

Having a housekeeper helped, but this is not what I envisioned as a committed wife and mother. I would tell my housekeeper, just entertain them for a few minutes so I can settle myself, and then I will play with them awhile. I wanted to manage my home, care for my children, and to make them my top priority. On the other hand, I loved my job, my salary, and the financial benefits that two salaries allowed us. But in the midst of it all, I knew that I had to make a decision.

Even though I decided to leave my job, and totally focus on my family, it was extremely difficult to make that move and tell my area manager. Then the thoughts of doubt came in like a flood. "Suppose I change my mind? Will we be able to make it on one salary? What will I do everyday, will I get bored? Then the Lord gave me a push and after about 15 minutes in the manager's office, it was done. As I walked out of the office, I felt free! I drove to the school to pick up my kids. And when I saw them running toward my open arms, I burst into tears because I knew without a shadow of doubt that I had made the right decision. Believing that this was God's will for my life, I moved forward in faith and obedience.

The change in my home and family as a result of this decision was amazing. There was a change in my husband, my children, and myself. We were all more relaxed; we became even closer, and really began to enjoy life as a family. We ate dinner together most evenings, before running down to the beach, or just having some fun in the back yard. To my amazement, our financial situation also improved. Many husbands have to stop at the donut shop in the morning to have a cup of coffee, but when his wife is a homemaker, he can get a better meal at home and save the $400.00 that he would have spent over the 365 days of the year just buying coffee. A year later, the Lord birthed the desire in our hearts to minister to other marriages. This is something I knew could not have been done if I was still on the job.

Even though many may not admit it, balancing a home, motherhood, a marriage life, and full-time job is almost impossible. It is difficult for a woman to fill all of these positions simultaneously, and be successful. Something or someone will have to suffer and in the majority of cases, it is the home. The home, which encompasses her marriage, her family, and her soul, bears the brunt of this loss. Managing a home is a full time business vocation, and a woman needs time to prepare herself for this task like any other. A good night's rest, a strong body, and a relaxed mind, are all required for the job.

As a homemaker, her day should always begin with time in prayer. Before rising each morning, she should spend time in prayer and later after seeing her husband off to work and the children off to school; she should devote some additional time in prayer before going about her daily chores. This puts her in a frame of mind that will set the pace for the rest of the day. It is during this time of prayer and devotion that she brings everything that concerns her before the Lord, including her husband and his job, her children, their friends, school, and teachers.

She should also pray for strength and wisdom and other needs in her family, church, community, and nation. When this is done she can move about her home with a happy heart, putting things in order. She may want to share an encouraging word, or pray with a neighbor in need. It could be someone that may be ill, someone that is shut in, or even spend some time with a good friend. She might even decide to have lunch with her husband.

By mid afternoon when the children come home from school, she is there to hug, and hold them, enjoy a game, favorite book, or share time together in the back yard. Time is available to teach her daughter to cook, or share a valuable lesson with her son. This is the advantage the homemaker has: time.

We must get back to the place that God has designed us to bloom in. Over the past decades, women have proven to themselves and men that they have the potential to be anything they want to be, from clerk or plumber to corporate leaders. We have taken over nations, churches, and more, but taking on these extra challenges have robbed us of many more meaningful things that have been entrusted to our care.

Hints for the Homemaker

- The ball is in her court; her biggest challenge will be discipline and time management. Her position is one where she basically works without supervision; therefore her ability to be self-motivated is extremely important. This calls for organization, planning, strategy, creativity, and commitment.

- A good idea is to organize a timetable according to your commitments. You may be a woman with infants, young children, or no children at all. Every homemaker's schedule is different. Using every minute is crucial.

- Use early morning hours to make a healthy breakfast for your husband and children. Time can be allocated for simple lessons in cleanliness, for example: teaching your child to make his/her bed, brushing teeth, dressing properly, putting together an outfit, and putting away their clothes.

- Devotions can be done as early as you want. It could be in the wee hours of the morning, just before the family awakes, or maybe after everyone leaves for work or school. However it is essential to begin your day committing everything to the Lord in prayer.

- Morning hours are generally set for tidying up and making the house feel clean and bright. During the middle of the day, you might have a free hour or break. This is a good time to take a leisurely bath, and freshen up after your housework is done, so that you can be refreshed when everybody gets home.

- Free hours can be used for lunch with a friend, getting beauty treatments, hosting your hubby to an unusual lunch break, or just a special time of relaxation. Participation in school activities, e.g. field trips, class visitation, shopping, crafts etc. can also be a pleasant treat.

- Avoid getting caught up in television and unnecessary phone calls, they will steal your time. Consider yourself at work for the Lord, your family, and yourself.

- It would be profitable to get cooking done during the early afternoon before the smaller children come home so that you can spend time with them or take them to extra-curricular activities. Upon returning dinner is ready for all. Mothers of teenage daughters may opt to prepare dinner during late afternoon to teach her daughter *or son* to help with cooking or share a few family secrets.

- As for those homemakers who work outside of the home, for you the name of the game is preparation. It helps to plan your family meals on weekends. You can also use off days like Sunday to cook enough for two days' meal. Before freezing meats, season them first to save time during the week in cooking.

- There were many evenings when I worked outside my home that I would prepare two meals at one time. The next morning while I prepared for work, I would partially cook the extra dish, and then refrigerate it for later. This would allow me additional time that evening.

- After dinner is a quiet time for relaxation, homework, or if you have a church or social meeting, you are free. It is a good practice in any relationship to come into agreement whenever possible about the things that are important in everyday life. For example daily church services are good, but consult your spouse to make certain that this schedule is good for all. An occasional evening out for the homemaker can give hubby an opportunity to spend time with the kids.

- Assign chores for your children that will increase with age and maturity. It is good that children of school age be given a bedtime between 8:00-9:30 p.m. to receive the required rest, and to allow parents a few extra hours alone before their bedtime.

- Homemakers are often not weary at night; Chores are done during the day, therefore evenings are often free of clutter. They are ready and prepared to spend quality time with their husbands. Remember he was not home all day, so in the early evenings give him a chance to relax alone, and later he is all yours.

12. A Meek & Quiet Spirit

I awoke one Saturday morning to the ringing of my bedside telephone. When I answered, the caller pleasantly offered me a product, but I declined gracefully. He went on to apologize for calling so early in the morning. I assured him that it was no problem because I had intended to get up early to pray. Then I asked him what time it was. "It's seven o'clock", he said. Then I realized that the voice became very gentle saying "That's right my child, get up and pray."

I jumped out of bed, but not before realizing that my phone was disconnected, and it was all a dream. I looked at the clock and realized it was indeed 7:00 a.m., the exact time I wanted to get up and pray. I believe it was the Holy Spirit that awoke me. Nonetheless, the dream left an impression upon me because the voice was so gentle, so reassuring. All that day I thought about what had happened, but more than that I could not get past the voice in my dream. It left an impression in my spirit. It was so tender, so peaceful, I thought to myself, "Could this be a glimpse of the softer side of God secured in the woman."

One of the most alluring essences of a lady is her sweet and gentle nature. This is what accentuates the real beauty of a female. The characteristic of her gracefulness, a meek spirit, her soft laughter, all mirror the part of God that makes the female so wonderfully attractive. Peter speaks of this hidden person of the heart, that meek and quiet spirit that makes a woman so precious. It begins from within and emanates to the outside. In communicating it can make such a difference. A woman may say to her child, "Bring that here this minute," in a rather coarse and condescending way or she can say soothingly "bring that for me quickly." It can mean the difference of a lifetime because children are so greatly affected by the words that they hear. Many times women believe that they have to be coarse or hard to get results. They watch how the masculine nature operates, and attempt to model him. But the nature of the man is out of place in the mannerisms of a woman.

Every woman wants to be beautiful, yet so many neglect the natural essence of the woman that makes her attractive. Physical beauty is fleeting, and can be marred at any moment, but the true beauty that comes from within will last forever. The negative force of feminism has stripped many women of their most precious assets without even realizing it. Desiring to appear strong, many women have embraced an unnatural masculine demeanor.

When we look at the coming fashions, it seems women are being drawn away from the look of femininity. In action, adornment, and speech, a lot of women are becoming more masculine. I remember meeting a young woman working on a construction site. She was dressed in overalls and covered with cement and dirt, struggling to lift a load of cement blocks. In times past, men would never pass a woman by and not help her. They honored her femininity, but today things are different.

There are women who are offended if one implies that they cannot do a man's job. Society has so warped their way of thinking that many struggle to prove that they can do just what a man can do. While it is possible for her to do a "man's" job, it is not always profitable to her. She has been created for a different purpose and her equality does not come from doing what men do.

It is important that we as women preserve the meekness of our spirit, a quality that makes us females. However, a meek heart should not be mistaken for a weak heart. The spirit of meekness is one of brokenness and humility. It produces a gentle heart that God can easily guide. Matthew 5:5 says, "Blessed are the meek for they shall inherit the earth."

When I was growing up, there was a female evangelist in our church that I considered the epitome of a godly woman. She was graceful and womanly in the way she spoke, dressed, and conducted herself. Her name was Barbara Williams. The only time I saw a stronger side of her was when God used her to minister to the church. She was like a lamb, but when she preached, she was like a lion.

To me, it was awesomely beautiful. She would preach the word with authority, and it would make you wonder how a woman who appeared so humble could expound the word in such a manner. Many female ministers strive to be rough and tough when all they need to be is a woman of God in every sense of the word. There exists a side of God that is likened to the lamb, and another that is likened to a lion. They are both attributes of God.

When it is time for the lion to present itself, God will show up in awesome power and authority. Conversely, the lamb, the docile nature of God will exhibit meekness and humility. When the woman walks in the spirit of meekness, she shows off the feminine side of God that is tender, sweet and compassionate. This is the attractive side of the creator that is very inviting and beautiful.

Outward adorning is also an important part of the woman of God. Her dress code should not bring attention to the flesh, but to the spirit. While in the mall recently, I questioned a sales lady about nice feminine dresses for my teenager. It seemed all that was being offered were pants, short skirts and other apparel that I didn't particularly want my daughter wearing. The lady said to me, "Well, we have to buy what sells." I began to look around, and take notice of things. The fashions were so revealing and lacking in modesty, outfits I would not want for my youngster.

In the church, the customary dress code has also changed drastically. A few years ago a woman ministering the word of God would not be caught in pants in the pulpit, whether she was singing, praying, or exhorting. Many say pants are comfortable. While the wearing of pants is not a sin, it is not the most feminine attire for a woman. We must be very careful in the way we adorn ourselves, especially as we present ourselves to other as a representation of Jesus Christ. Our standard for dressing must be set by our godly conscience, and not by Hollywood designers.

One woman admitted that when she wore slacks, she sometimes felt manly, and there is much truth behind this. There is an attitude that presents itself with the wearing of various clothing. Dressed in a mini or short skirt a woman may feel very sexy or flirtatious. In an evening gown, she tends to feel queenly, elegant and beautiful. Adorned in an expensive outfit there is a sense of affluence. In shorts, she may feel active or playful, and in pants she may feel mannish and brave. A woman would not likely sit with her legs ajar in a dress, but in pants, almost anything goes.

The word of God admonishes the godly woman how to appropriately adorn her self (1 Peter 3). She should take steps to be well covered, discreet, and presentable, in a manner suitable for the feminine look of a woman. Her adornment is a representation of what and who she is.

A Policeman is respected because of who he is, especially when he is dressed in his uniform. If he wore plain clothing he could easily be mistaken for just about anyone. In fact, he may wear plain clothing to trick criminals into letting down their guards so he can catch them. However a uniformed police demands respect. Likewise, when a woman adorns herself in a godly manner, she gains the respect of those around her.

When the Spirit of God began dealing with me on this issue, I began sharing it with other women and found that what he was saying to me was indeed being said to others. Beware! While the inward adornment is extremely important, the outward appearance must also be taken care of.

Many young girls today reject the feminine look, because they consider it old-fashioned. We experienced this firsthand when we moved from the Bahamas to Florida. My two daughters wore uniforms to school all of their lives.. So they gladly wore dresses for the first few weeks of school, and then getting dressed each morning became an issue. To me, the way the other little girls dressed looked so boyish, but to my daughters, it was "cool." But I stuck to my standards and advised my daughters against it. As a Christian, I knew that it was important that my daughters should reflect that they reared in a home where Christ was the center. If anything, they should set the example for their peers to follow.

Within weeks, my daughter came home and said, "Mom you know a lot of my friends are beginning to wear dresses like me, so I guess it is alright." Whew! Sometimes it can be a fight, but as parents we must take authority, especially when we stand as the most impressive role model our children have. The part of the role model is very important to the upkeep of the godly standards of future generations. Young people are crying out for hope, for direction, for someone not only to tell, but to show them an alternative to what they see around them.

A meek and quiet spirit is the most attractive spirit that a woman can have. It is attractive to God and to her husband and to those with whom she comes in contact with. It is attractive because it seeks to serve rather than control. It disarms the argumentative and belligerent attitudes as it seeks to bring peace through humility and grace. Be encouraged, meekness is the greatest asset that you can have because it invokes the favor or God.

13. Highly Favored

The calling of motherhood, homemaker, and femininity are powerful tools placed in the lives of women. When these are diminished in any way, we cannot truly fulfill our purpose as women. But God is able to repair, and restore that which he has created. If we ever seem to fall short, we need only to say, "Lord show me how to become what you have ordained me to be." We must focus our attention on being, not who we think we are, or who others may think we are, but exactly what God has created us to be.

My mind goes to the beginning of time to Cain and Abel. God required of them both to offer up a sacrifice. Abel's sacrifice was received while Cain's was rejected. Reason: one brought a sacrifice to the Lord that was pleasing through his obedience, the other brought a sacrifice that ***he thought*** the Lord would be pleased with. As mothers today, how would God respond to our offering to him through our children, our husbands, and our faith? Would he be pleased with our sacrifice? Would he be pleased with our desire to build his kingdom? The psalmist, David said, "The fruit of the womb is his reward." How precious is this reward? Does it demand the best that you have to give? In Genesis 3:16 God told us that the responsibility of the woman would not be easy, but cause for much sorrow.

The New Testament book of 1st Timothy shows us that if we are faithful to his word, God will make a way of escape for us. Notwithstanding, the woman shall be saved in childbearing, if she continues in faith, charity, and holiness with sobriety (1 Tim 3:15). This is the promise of God. Satan knows that if he can deceive her into satisfying herself first, and putting her needs before that of God, she will destroy her seed.

The word of God states in John 15:7 "If you abide in me, and my word abides in you, then ye shall ask what you will and it shall be given to you." If women would come into obedience with God's word, there is nothing that God would withhold from them. All that is required of us as women is an act of faith. God has made a way of escape for all of us. His Holy Spirit is with us to show us how to fulfill the destiny of our lives. He is unique, and so are we. We need not compare ourselves with anyone else, or try to live up to what God is doing in other women's lives, because the spirit of God that lives in each of us will make us what we ought to be. If allowed, he will make our calling, ministry, husband, children, home, and heart as unique and beautiful as he is.

My prayer is that God will open your eyes to the divine purpose for your life, and that you would be obedient to his word. The things of this life are temporary; therefore we must strive for that which is eternal. The lives of our husbands and children can indeed be touched for all eternity. May God Bless You Richly!

Part Four

Understanding Why We Fuss & Fight

Introduction

The Bible says, *"In the multitude of words there wanteth not sin: but he that refraineth his lips is wise." (Proverbs 10:19)*; paraphrased: the more you talk, the more there is a potential of saying something wrong or injurious to another. How powerful! However, in the average marriage, we are yet to tame our tongues.

Indeed, the art of verbal mastery is a lifelong experience...but it can be learned! In this section, the principles of verbal maturity in marriage are outlined. With due diligence and humble hearts, we can save our marriages from the pain and emotional turmoil that result from unnecessary arguing and bickering.

We invite you to patiently and attentively turn the pages of Part Four and allow the Lord to change your heart and mind. Your mouth need not be a lethal weapon of oppression or depression; let it become rather an instrument of grace that uplifts and nurtures the hearers. Let it become rather an instrument of grace that uplifts and nurtures the hearers. *"Let your speech be always with grace, seasoned with salt, that ye may know how ye ought to answer every man." (Colossians 4:6)*

But let it be the hidden man of the heart, in that which is not corruptible, even the ornament of a meek and quiet spirit, which is in the sight of God of great price.
—1 Peter 3:4

14. Pressures & Problems

The annoying sound of the loud siren had stopped, but the red and yellow lights continued to flash as the police officers stood talking to the couple in the quiet countryside community. In the stillness of the quiet evening with only the occasional sound of a hooting owl, one could hear the sobs of a distressed female. Nina, a petite middle-aged woman, body quivered with emotion as she spoke.

On the porch, her stout husband, John, related his version of events to the skinny male police officer. It was the end of the month and sales were at an all time low. In fact, his entire office had been under tremendous pressure because out of forty-five sales agents, not one had made the company's quota. He had stopped at the dry cleaners to pick up clothes that had been there for much too long, before making his way home.

When he stepped into the house, he was met with the enraged voice of his wife. The cell phones had been disconnected and she was furious. *"What are you doing with the money,* she screamed! *Every day you leave for work, but I don't see the results of your labor. You know John, my mother said, 'I need to go to work in order to save this family because you are doing absolutely nothing.' I am sick and tired of this,"* she shouted.

John stopped. *"Sir, I passed right by her, I didn't want to say anything for fear of starting this kind of scene, but she just kept on, and on with her accusations."* The Officer continued to take notes and nodded for John to continue.

"But, Nina was just getting started, and again she yelled, 'Look at you, you can't even defend yourself, or maybe you have gone dumb. Can you hear me John, you need to be a man in this house or I will begin wearing your pants for you. John, say something or I will call the minister to cast that dumb and deaf spirit out of you, and then you will be able to respond to me.'

She went on to say, 'Boy, I should have listened to my mother and marry Lester, the doctor, or Phil the banker, why did I have to fall in love with the likes of you!' Then, as I walked into the kitchen, she proceeded to follow me, so I turned and said, 'Listen Nina, to hell with you and your mother, I have had a hard day and the last thing I need is to have both of you on my back.' But, I guess I said the wrong thing again, I was just so worn out, that's when she threatened to leave. 'Well if that's the way you feel I will spend the night at my mother's house."

John went on as the officer continued to write up the report. *"That was the last thing I needed, I was tired of her mouth. I was hungry because I didn't have any breakfast or lunch that day."* Straying a bit to for emphasis, John interjected, *"She doesn't make breakfast for me anymore."*

He Continued, *"She just kept mouthing. I tried to stop her, but she would not listen to me. I told her she was not making the situation any better and that she should stay home and do what she was supposed to do. But that sent her upstairs to pack her things. In record time she was back downstairs with her overnight bag in her hand. My heart was racing and I reached out to stop her, that's when she pushed me against the counter. That's when I, aaaa... I hit her. I watched as she fell to the ground from the weight of my hand against her face. I didn't intend to hit her, I don't abuse my wife, but I was just.... I don't know...fed up, I guess. Immediately I felt disgusted for what I had done, at that point I turned away and walked into the den."*

The officer stopped writing for a while, as he looked over to where Nina and the female officer sat talking. His stare was interrupted as John began to talk again. *"Lately, we have been getting into arguments almost every other day, because things are so tight around here I guess. I know she deserved better, and I am guilty because I can't give it to her, but I am trying my best on this job. Things just aren't the way they used to be. Usually, I am able to simply walk away, or totally ignore her, but today it seemed more than I could take."*

John was quiet for a moment before he commented again, *"And her mother, Lord, her mother, she is our biggest problem, I blame her, officer, for putting thoughts in my wife's head. I heard them talking after this situation, she told my wife to call the cops, and have me arrested, because she could do a better job of taking care of my family."* After saying this, John rested his head in his hand and wept. The officer shifted from one leg to another, he did not know what to say next. This was his third response to domestic violence for the day and he was just as baffled. Why so much fussing and fighting?

Many couples ask themselves this same question. Why the constant arguing? Who is right and who should just shut-up? Indeed, resolving conflicts has become the central focus of counseling offices. Without peace in the house, separation and divorce will eventually walk in and take up residence.

It may start with a very simple or trivial matter. However, these simple things usually become major battles that wreck marriages and relationships. As the saying goes, "It is the small foxes that destroy the vines." Most people when they hear the word, or think of conflict, imagine a big fight, or violent confrontation, but conflict can be as simple as going against the flow of things. One person may favor things one way, while the other may prefer something different. This is the basis of a conflict. It can be verbal, physical, mental, or emotional, however, it is when rage and anger, hidden in a desire for control sets in, that the conflict often becomes violent.

The Bible says, *"Only by pride cometh contention: but with the well advised is wisdom." (Proverbs 13:10)* At the root of ungodly conflicts is a spirit of pride: a desire to dominate another or a desire to have one's own way in spite of conditions that forbid it. If we remember this, we would be well on our way to working through unnecessary conflicts and even avoiding them.

We live in an atmosphere of constant stress and pressure. Coupled with this, is the insatiable desire for more and more things, leaving no room for our spiritual man to grow or develop. As a result, we don't have the wisdom or the will to overcome the conflicts and problems that come our way.

Like Alice, we are in Wonderland and deep fantasy. Our relationships are suffering and our families are upside down because of unresolved issues. In most cases, it is not even the issue at hand, but our selfish hearts wanting their own way; selfishness and greed that will eventually drown us in bitterness and unforgiveness.

However, this need not be our case. What we must keep foremost in our minds is conflicts are a part of life. Conflicts are allowed by God so that we can pray and grow in faith and wisdom as we learn to trust God in the most difficult of circumstances. Like the scripture says, *"These things I have spoken unto you, that in me ye might have peace. In the world ye shall have tribulation: but be of good cheer; I have overcome the world." (John 16:33)*

15. Having a Good Fight

"Brethren, if a man be overtaken in a fault ye which are spiritual <u>restore such a one in the spirit of meekness; considering thyself, lest thou also be tempted.</u> Bear ye one another's burdens, and so fulfill the law of Christ." (Galatians 6:1-2)

"A soft answer turneth away wrath: but grievous words stir up anger." (Proverbs 15:1)

"But speaking the truth in love may grow up into him in all things, which is the head, even Christ." (Ephesians 4:15)

It was the sweet first year of our marriage and along with all the areas of adjustment and growth, there were a few clashes. I remember a few months after our wedding, we were arguing over something or the other. Suddenly, my husband said, "That's it." I watched as he pulled a suitcase from the closet and proceeded to put a few of my things inside. With that he walked to the door and rested the suitcase at the front door. This literally shocked me, because my hubby was not a very confrontational person, always keeping it cool.

Back then, if our conflict was not resolved quickly he would take our dog, Freedom, and jog to the beach. When he got back he was in a better frame of mind to talk about whatever the issue was. On the other hand, I preferred to deal with situations first, then go for a walk. So this time when he said to me, if you cannot abide by what I say, then I am sending you back home until you make up your mind what you want, because I am not going to be constantly fussing over this or that.

As I stood looking, I could not believe my eyes or ears. Thoughts raced through my mind. What is up with this man, he has got to be joking? Would he really let me go? Am I pushing him too far? After a long hour of silence, he came into the room where I was sitting alone, (I was probably wondering why I didn't call his bluff and see if he would really let me go,) but when he came and put his arms around me everything was fine.

We then sat together, and we were able to talk quietly. I told him the older men in the church that were giving him advice about how to deal with a young wife had missed it, so he had better seek God for personal advice with me. He promised me he would get rid of their how-to advice and start over. Later, we went out to get some ice cream cones and walk on the beach, at peace again. We had come to a place of reconciliation realizing that while we wanted satisfaction, we also wanted to be at peace with each other.

Because of this, we were willing to put our personal desires aside for the sake of being reconciled back to each other. I thought to myself, "This must be how the Lord feels when a sinner or backslider repents and is reconciled back to Him. Indeed, a conflict resolved peacefully is like healing balm to a marriage. When a conflict is resolved in this manner, it touches all areas of the marriage. Trust is restored, tensions dissipate, and even the lovemaking climbs a notch.

However, for the inexperienced, and for most married couples, conflicts usually end on a sour note. They end with shouting, fault-finding, character assassinations, and unforgiveness. Few partners find the keys that lock the door to unforgiveness and open the door to peace and reconciliation.

I believe that one crucial mistake made by spouses is that of demonization. Yes, I know a lot of time it's the Devil at work, but we must take care never to demonize an individual. When we criticize a person with negative words and a condescending tone, we invite a defensive rebuttal.

This is never a good strategy and will always bring poor results. Remember, you love the other person. Yes, they have irritated you through their poor habits and repeat offenses, however, your desire is reconciliation and reconnection, and not for them to give up in despair after a tongue lashing. Demonizing your partner will do this.

When a positive approach is used, there is greater possibility of a favorable outcome. You see, when you approach someone with respect, courtesy, and the spirit of love, it's easier to disarm a bad response. The purpose of someone giving a bad response is usually to return the favor of "pride bruising". In other words, "Okay, you wanna go there....let's get down and dirty," or "You hurt me, I will hurt you back!"

However, if you have watered the ground of conversation with the gentle and kind approach, it doesn't leave much room or opportunity for the other partner to sow seeds of bitterness and anger. This is the good fight that you must strive to have.

The good fight is when we confront a situation not to point out someone's poor character faults so that we can look good, rather, it's, "let us work together for mutual benefit." For example, your husband is neither thrifty nor conscientious when spending the family's money. To insult and demean him for being an idiot or moron will not help him, but disarm him in his ability to fight against his weakness. Your words of offense can cause him to become bitter instead of fostering a desire to face and correct his problem.

First, recognize that you are in this together. His failings will impact the family and your pocket book. Conversely, you're in a win, win, situation if you can help him to see the error of his ways in a tactful and loving manner. This may begin by sharing how you have personally overcome similar struggles and now benefit from those mistakes. This humble approach usually gets a good response from even the most obstinate person.

In the early stages of our marriage, my wife and I experienced our share of conflicts. In most cases, we were simply trying to get the other person to yield to 'my way'. There were times I would say, "I believe that God wants us to do this or that" in turn pointing out the error of my wife's ways. This was self-righteous manipulation. So, if I didn't get my way....**Goddddd** was being disobeyed!!

Kim, on the other hand would not fight against that for fear of going against what God wanted. Nonetheless, there were times she would stand up to me. "God speaks to me too," she said at one point

"And he is not telling me that!" I felt at times that she feared submission. Or worse, she feared that some of my advice would bring disaster. We had yet to learn how to have a good fight. It wasn't until life threw us some hard blows that we learned to confront our battles together.

When our last baby died from SIDS only two and a half months after birth, it brought a lot of change to our marriage. I climbed into a hole of depression not wanting to talk, while Kim anxiously sought comfort from me and others. This, of course, brought tension and crisis to our marriage.

We were handling our grief differently, and it was straining our relationship. One afternoon, we decided to take a walk on the beach to relieve some tension. Kicking sand and slowly making our way along the shore, we talked candidly for the first time. We each expressed our thoughts. It wasn't easy. The tension would surface every now and then as we made our point, but it was a beginning.

It was then that we realized that when we fought badly, we had to work hard to climb out our holes of bitterness and unforgiveness. If we handled our crisis properly, we learned, we grew, and our marriage matured. Having a good fight was not easy, but it was the only way to heal and move on.

16. Drop the Bags...Honey!

"Be ye angry, and sin not: let not the sun go down upon your wrath." (Ephesians 4:26)

"And when ye stand praying, forgive, if ye have aught against any: that your Father also which is in heaven may forgive you your trespasses. But if ye do not forgive, neither will your Father which is in heaven forgive your trespasses." (Mark 11:25-26)

"But I say unto you, Love your enemies, bless them that curse you, do good to them that hate you, and pray for them which despitefully use you, and persecute you;" (Matthew 5:44)

"<u>Dearly beloved, avenge not yourselves,</u> but rather give place unto wrath: for it is written, Vengeance is mine; I will repay, saith the Lord. Therefore if thine enemy hunger, feed him; if he thirst, give him drink: for in so doing thou shalt heap coals of fire on his head. <u>Be not overcome of evil, but overcome evil with good.</u>" (Romans 12:19-21)

There is nothing as destructive and un-raveling to a marriage relationship as unforgiveness. Whether it's offenses between spouses or an offense that happened years before a marriage was consummated, unforgiveness is like cancer that eventually spreads to all areas of the marriage.

Let me give you an example of a case that I became familiar with. A young lady and her husband were having tremendous problems in their marriage. There were constant arguments and heated exchanges. The husband complained that his wife would "blow up" over the simplest of situations and refused to honor his leadership in the home.

After numerous counseling sessions, their marriage only grew worse. The case was referred to me and after investigation; I discovered that this young lady was verbally abused by her father. She had never forgiven her father, and as a result, hatred of males developed in her heart. This unforgiveness was the root of their marital problems; and forgiveness, the only way forward.

Most of the offenses that we experience in life may not be our fault, however, it's always the response that makes the difference. For some people, minor offenses are forgivable, but major offenses are not to be forgiven, or forgiveness withheld for a time. If this were the case, none of us could ever receive the unmerited forgiveness of God. God has forgiven us freely and without reservation.

Yet, most of us continue to hold on to old wounds. For me, it was my father abandoning me when I was six months old, the times he didn't show at my graduation, and wedding. He was always showing up at other family member's important dates but not mine. I waited for the moment to just let him have it.

When I got the moment, I told him. "Where you when I needed you most?" "Where were you, dad?" Of course, he just muttered some lame explanation that didn't ease the pain of rejection or give weight to his excuse. My unforgiveness over the years was still not dealt with. I was still hurting after our confrontation.

It was the Lord's healing balm that cured me. It was his grace that gave me the power to forgive and move on. I love my father now; not because he has been such a great Dad, rather it's because the love of God resides in my heart; a love that is unconditional; a love that "loves" in spite of the past.

A young man who grew up in the tough parts of the Chicago gave me some potent and sobering advice. He said that he had been acquainted with some of the toughest guys in Chicago; guys that have done some of the most heinous crimes including murder. He said that when one of them told him that revenge was not worth it, he was a bit intrigued and wanted to understand why.

He said that the tough guy told him that he had taken revenge on people but the thrill of getting even lasted for only a moment, however, after that, depression sets in. And depression leads you down a deep, dark hole where you question and regret the things that you have done. He said that the tough guy told him that it is far better to work through a situation or problem that you have with someone rather than seek revenge.

Wow! If only we so-called civilized folks can understand. Unforgiveness is poison. It's poisoning yourself!! You can't change the past, you have no power over the future, yet you brood, question and hate the person that offended you. This can change nothing. It will only take you deeper and deeper into depression and delusion.

The only way out of unforgiveness is to drop the bags of poison. Get rid of it!!! Run into the arms of mercy.....like a song writer so ably put forth "I'm running...I'm running...I'm running to the Mercy Seat. I'm running to the Mercy Seat where Jesus is calling...." We all need the mercy of God to burst our bags of unforgiveness. Only He, the Lord Jesus, can lift the weight that keeps us in bondage to pass hurts and wounds.

In my marriage, I found myself slipping into unforgiveness without even realizing it. When Kim would do something I didn't like, I would sometime go to bed angry or pout for days just wanting to punish her for her disobedience or lack of respect. This didn't change things; prayers did. Taking matters into your own hands will always bring disastrous results.

Our alarming divorce rates and dysfunctional families are largely the result of unforgiveness. Unresolved issues that lead to bitterness, hatred and eventually revenge, yet, the question is how we can combat unforgiveness before it becomes a problem and takes over our lives? For most people, the very thing that they want to avoid is what they need to do. Take the humble road. **You can only overcome evil with good.** That's the only way!! You must combat the evil of unforgiveness with humility and love. The Bible puts in this way, *"If thine enemy be hungry, give him bread to eat; and if he be thirsty, give him water to drink: For* *thou shalt heap coals of fire upon his head, and the LORD shall reward thee." (Proverbs 25:21-22)*

Does this mean that we should be a doormat for people to use and abuse? No. However, our response to evil should never be revenge, if we hope to heal and be renewed through God's grace. Doing good to evil people brings a third power into the equation: the All-powerful, All-mighty God. He can defeat and overcome anything and anyone.

That's why we should be quick to forgive; especially, if you want to stay above the water of depression and heartache. At the root of unforgiveness is pride. I'm right and you're wrong. I'm righteous and you're unrighteous. In other words, I have the right to hold my offense against you. This is the message that is heralded on the major talk shows that lead people into a deep hole that is almost impossible to get out of.

To take it a step further, our ability to forgive is directly proportional to the level of pride in our lives. Pride blinds us to our own faults. We can only see the wrong that was done to us. So we resort to the blame game, taking vengeance on the offending party, and withholding forgiveness. However, if we are humble in spirit, we recognize our own failures and God's abundant mercy upon us. We also see life from a different perspective, knowing that it's only God's grace and mercy that keeps us from offending others. With this in mind, we can forgive freely and without reservation.

Jesus' parable about an unforgiving servant illustrates the point of God unmerited forgiveness to us and our need to forgive others:

"Jesus saith unto him, I say not unto thee, Until seven times: but, Until seventy times seven. Therefore is the kingdom of heaven likened unto a certain king, which would take account of his servants. And when he had begun to reckon, one was brought unto him, which owed him ten thousand talents. But forasmuch as he had not to pay, his lord commanded him to be sold, and his wife, and children, and all that he had, and payment to be made. The servant therefore fell down, and worshiped him, saying, Lord, have patience with me, and I will pay thee all. Then the lord of that servant was moved with compassion and loosed him, and forgave him the debt. But the same servant went out, and found one of his fellow servants,

which owed him a hundred pence: and he laid hands on him, and took him by the throat, saying, Pay me that thou owest. And his fellow servant fell down at his feet, and besought him, saying, Have patience with me, and I will pay thee all.

And he would not: but went and cast him into prison, till he should pay the debt. So when his fellow servants saw what was done, they were very sorry, and came and told unto their lord all that was done. Then his lord, after that he had called him, said unto him, O thou wicked servant, I forgave thee all that debt, because thou desiredst me: Shouldest not thou also have had compassion on thy fellow servant, even as I had pity on thee? And his lord was wroth, and delivered him to the tormentors, till he should pay all that was due unto him." So likewise shall my heavenly **Father do also unto you, if ye from your hearts forgive not every one his brother their trespasses.** *" (Matthew 18:23-35)*

Unforgiveness can be very tormenting, as you regret and revisit the crime that was done to you, the depression and oppression continues in your life. I want to make a point for those people who always use an abusive situation to substantiate unforgiveness, revenge and divorce. Always, in an abusive situation one should always look for a safe haven. Maybe a safe haven is at the parent's house or in another state/town or even out of the country. However, abuse is not the unpardonable sin. In fact, we have all been abusive in our lives at some time or the other.

Bullying someone in school is abuse. Forcing someone to do what we want whether by deliberate actions or manipulation is abuse. In fact, mental abuse is one of the worse forms of abuse if we use words purposely or in ignorance to demean someone else. Who has been guilty of abuse? All of us. Maybe not as grievous as the violent physical abuser, but we have done it. If we have all been guilty, then, shouldn't we all forgive?

If anyone had the right to be unforgiving, it was Jesus. Falsely accused and brutally abused by his captors, he forgave them without question, as he suffered innocently on the cross. **The Scribes, Pharisees, and Romans all deserved the utter indignation of the Lord. Instead, he said, "Father, forgive them for they know not**

what they do." (Luke 23:24) Does this means he justified their abuse. No, not in the least. If his abusers never repented of their actions, they would die in their sins and face the judgment of the same Lord who said, "Father, forgive them."

Handling Rejection

But what happens if you reach out for reconciliation and the other person rejects you? Although, forgiving frees us from stress and emotional pain, it is never a guarantee that reconciliation will work or the other party will change. It simply opens the door.

Time and patience will prove whether the other party will change. This, we must leave completely to God. However, there are some things that we can do to effect reconciliation. We can verbally express our forgiveness to the offending party. Demonstrate in our actions that we have forgiven them.

With the door open for reconciliation, we must move forward in faith. Remember, forgiveness releases us from the burden of an unpaid debt. And, it is the way to true spiritual freedom and healing. This is why we have to drop the bags! If we don't drop the bags, we are setting not only ourselves up for failure, but our marriages as well.

17. Exercising Control

"But he that is married careth for the things that are of the world, how he may please his wife. There is difference also between a wife and a virgin. The unmarried woman careth for the things of the Lord, that she may be holy both in body and in spirit: but she that is married careth for the things of the world, how she may please her husband." (1 Corinthians 7:33-34)

"Let nothing be done through strife or vain glory; but <u>in lowliness of mind let each esteem other better than themselves.</u>" (Philippians 2:3)

<u>Marriage above everything is a platform for service.</u> The institution of marriage is a lifelong establishment where you learn to serve and meet the needs of another person unconditionally. If you got married for any other reason, you have missed the mark. As the above scripture indicate, husband and wife are to zealously seek to please one another.

Usually, we do this during dating and courtship. We buy gifts. We are unselfish with our time, and we consistently put our best foot forward. However, after marriage, it changes for most people. We've got what we wanted and now we can just lay back and enjoy the goods. This leaves a vacuum in the relationship that usually leads to control and manipulation.

In other words, if you can't get what you want then you better get it by hook or crook. Whether it's money, sex or power, exercising control is a means of getting your way in the marriage, and, usually at the expense of the marriage itself.

At the root of control is the spirit of fear and insecurity wrapped up in pride. Fear that things will not work out; faithless in God's ability and power, and the need to put on a face of confidence and self-assurance. Eventually, we sink into a life of hypocrisy to cover-up our inner failure.

We become abusive and deceptive as we treat our mates and others with apathy and lack of respect. Driven by fear and pride, we can only see the need to get our way blinded to the fact that we are hurting others. Our only hope is true repentance and humbleness of heart.

However, people who operate with a spirit of control, always defend themselves because they see humility and repentance as losing and being disrespected. In other words, they always have to be on the top. They feed on the need to feel superior and better.

Intellectual Control

This is an area many men are challenged in, including me. I can think back to times when I thought I was more intelligent than Kim. As a result, I believed that I was qualified to make better decisions. Aanaanh!!! Wrong answer! Being intellectual smarter doesn't mean that you have the right to control or dominate a relationship. In fact, what I have learned is that the person who is least educated is more qualified for God's grace. They are not usually shackled by an arrogant attitude that resists the wisdom and direction of the Holy Spirit.

> *"But he giveth more grace. Wherefore he saith, God resisteth the proud, but giveth grace unto the humble." (James 4:6)*

> *"But God hath chosen the foolish things of the world to confound the wise; and God hath chosen the weak things of the world to confound the things which are mighty; And base things of the world, and things which are despised, hath God chosen, yea, and things which are not, to bring to naught things that are: That no flesh should glory in his presence." (1 Corinthians 1:27-29)*

When we use our so-call intellectual knowledge to whip people into submission, we set ourselves up for a fall. Knowledge is good if we use it in conjunction with the wisdom of God. However, if we showcase our knowledge to exalt ourselves over our spouses, or anyone else for that matter, we not only bruise their spirits with our arrogance, we disqualify ourselves from receiving God's help.

Intellectual control is a form of pride that blinds us from the simplicity of truth and pure wisdom. When we walk in intellectual pride, we ignore good advice and resist help because we believe that we "know." As a male man, I have experienced this in my own marriage as I ignored my wife's good advice sometime to the detriment of the whole family when I spent too much or ignored advice regarding people who I was dealing with. Yes, being "smart" can have its downfalls.

The key to using knowledge correctly is being a team player. Learn to listen and appreciate the advice that your husband or wife and others give you. This is not a license to be a headless chicken not taking charge or confidently doing things. A person who is afraid to take charge or lack confidence when doing things is equally as frustrating as an arrogant intellectual.

The healthy medium is confidence and sensitivity; confident enough not to be afraid of taking some risks, and sensitive enough to listen and take sound advice. This again, calls for a humble and submissive attitude.

Sexual Control

A lot of arguments happen because of sexual conflicts; especially when sex is used as a weapon and tool of control. For a man, sex can be a way of dominating his wife when it is forced upon her without romance or foreplay. This could result in resistance, rejection, and robotic behavior, as the wife begins to see sex as a duty instead of a treasured moment of love and affection with her husband.

There are also occasions when a woman, who sees the vulnerability of a man's strong sex drive, may withhold sex as a means of punishment or gaining control over her husband. This too brings confusion and strife in a marriage as the husband may realize love-making is reward instead of mutual pleasure. Scripture clearly teaches that using sex as a weapon of control is off limits to both husband and wife.

> *"The wife hath not power of her own body, but the husband: and likewise also the husband hath not power of his own body, but the wife. Defraud ye not one the other, except it be with consent for a time, that ye may give yourselves to fasting and prayer; and come together again, that Satan tempt you not for your incontinency."*
> (1 Corinthians 7:4-5)

The gift of lovemaking is a gift from God to the marriage relationship for nurturing, intimacy, inspiration, and procreation (childbearing). And it should never be abused or neglected. Husbands and wives who disobey this commandment open the door for evil spirits to attack the other party with sexual temptation. So beware!!

It is not always easy to leave sex outside of conflicts, because it begins in our minds and flows through the nerves in our bodies. I believe it is easier for a man to make love after a heated argument than for a woman because the male psyche is hot-wired to be easily aroused by what he sees. A woman usually has to be coached into the land of sexual fulfillment through words and touch.

Thus, husband and wife should always communicate their sexual feelings to their mates to avoid major conflicts. Tact and persuasion are the only antidote when things are going wrong. Whether it's an unromantic partner or marital stress arising from financial, job related, family problems and the like: **Talk about it.** Refusal to deal with problems at hand creates insecurities, and will rob your marriage of spontaneity and sweetness.

Monetary Control

> *"For the love of money is the root of all evil: which while some coveted after, they have erred from the faith, and pierced themselves through with many sorrows."* (1 Timothy 6:10)

There was a time not long ago when most bread-winners of the family were men. However, that has changed in our time, and especially in our western world. In fact, a lot of women are the major bread-winners in the family. Their salaries and position of power in the world have increased resulting in many problems in marriage about who is really the head, if the wife makes more money or has a better job, then, who should have the final say?

The truth is money usually showcases the insecurities in people's lives, and whether through plenty or little, it causes problems in the marriage. If that wasn't true then all rich people should have successful marriages and all poor people would be divorced. This we know to be untrue, in fact, a lot more poor people have successful marriages.

As in all things, when problems start we can usually trace them back to principles not being obeyed. The Bible teaches that the male man is the head of the family, and this puts the burden on him to provide adequately for his family. He was designed for this role both spiritually and physically and will not change until the end of our age or when the Lord comes to rule and reign.

However, the male man's role as head of the home and major bread-winner never excluded the gifts and talents of his wife, or her equality as his help-meet. This means that she can have her own business and assist with income if needed. Being the wife never relegated a woman to childbearing and childrearing. However, as indicated in Proverbs 28, when married, **her primary duty is to her husband and family.**

A lot of financial arguments can be avoided if husband and wives can operate more as a team rather than **married but living single (meaning you do things without consultation or being selfish with**

one's resources). Always move toward unity. However, this may take time as trust is built. Every marriage is different. There are Christian counselors who claim since you're married you should have one account.

I believe that we can work toward this, especially if only one person is the bread-winner. However, I believe that an account for the bills and individual accounts would work better. Only you know you bills and income. <u>Sit down work together always, **always**, considering the other person.</u>

Marriage calls for service. The man is to meet the needs of the woman and vice versa. Money in this equation is no different. The money is firstly to defray the family expenses no matter who makes it; then comes pleasure and personal interest. When either party decides to be selfish with their income, it causes strife and financial problems.

Money problems can develop from a myriad of reasons:

1. *Husband not providing adequately*
2. *Husband/wife spending too much on pleasure items*
3. *Both parties not conserving or being thrifty*
4. *Wife not doing her part to assist*
5. *In-laws or other family member interfering in the smooth flow of the financial income e.g. supporting another family member at the expense of one's own family*
6. *Use of drugs etc.*
7. *Sickness*

However, when they do surface, fussing and fighting will only compound them. Money problems require wisdom and thriftiness. Immediately stop doing things that "eat-up" the money. Anything that is called pleasure can be cut or eliminated all together if need be. Put a budget in place. Open an account for the bills. Pay your tithes and give a good offering and help people when you can (this brings the supernatural provision and the favor of God into your life and family).

Usually, when people have money problems, it's only the tip of the iceberg. Other problems of stubbornness, selfishness and pleasure centeredness are already in play. Repenting and eliminating these major problems will almost immediately result into financial and monetary relief.

Psychic Control

I believe that this type of control is the major control being used today in marriages; using words and situations to bring confusion and insecurities to the other mate so that they can be controlled. This type of control is especially used in the religious environment as people are **controlled by hype, emotion and deceit.**

While this book was being written, Warren Jeffs, a renowned polygamist, and leader of a Mormon cult in Southern Utah was found guilty of being an accomplice to rape. Mr. Jeffs, a self-proclaimed Prophet, used religious persuasion and manipulation to get hundreds of people to follow him. Using tapes, videos and other media, these people were daily treated to a steady dose of deceit; constantly telling them to listen and obey the Prophet (Mr. Jeffs being the Prophet).

But how can a person do this so successfully? The key to manipulation and control is fear and insecurity. When people are made to feel insecure about themselves, they can be easily controlled. Mr. Jeffs' followers had no self-esteem or personal value of themselves. Thus, their lives were simply to revolve around the Prophet.

In a marriage or any relationship, every one is an equal. We have been put on this earth to love and serve one another; not dominate and control. Our gifts, talents and position of authority are the things that make us different, however, God did not give us gifts and talents so that people can worship us.

Every gift and talent that we have is to point people to a wonderful and All-powerful God. Like Warren Jeffs, many people who have gifts use them to influence and dominate others. This is done especially in the religious environment and amounts to psychic control or what we in the religious community call witchcraft.

Psychic control can be done by any individual who we trust without question. Only God is to be trusted with all our heart and without question. All human beings are fallible and are only to be followed as long as they are following the ways of the Lord. God's ways are love, compassion, faith and truth.

When any person who we know departs from this, we must cease following them or risk becoming a part of their delusions and deceit. Many people, instead of standing up to deceit and delusion would rather compromise. And this is why psychic control is rampant during our time.

People compromise for many reasons: pleasure, money, favors, promotion, friendship, fear of rejection and the list goes on. Thus, they are willing to sell their souls rather than confront lies and deceit. People who live under psychic control live in constant fear and denial. They are afraid to face the truth and the fear that they feel.

This is the way cult leaders control others, and the same way psychic control is perpetrated in a marriage. A husband or wife who is under psychic control, would rather compromise for fear of rejection, or the wrath of the controller. This individual will often allow brutality, incest, refuse to confront pertinent issues, allow themselves to be treated without respect, and so on.

Breaking psychic control begins with facing and confronting your fears: the woman who is afraid of losing her husband's income, so she submits to brutal and demeaning treatment; the "yes dear" man who is afraid of rocking the boat because of his wife's scorn and sexual punishment. **Fear** must be faced and conquered, or the psychic control will continue.

Do not expect a person who uses psychic control over you to give up easily. In fact, these are the people who become violent because they are losing control. Seeking a safe haven (a place of refuge away and not known by the offender) may be your only recourse. Remember, your safety first, however, you can only break psychic control by confronting it.

Remember, any one in authority is deserving of respect and honor, however, they are never to achieve God-like status in our minds or hearts; not a spouse, child, your pastor, your bishop, your president...no one! *"Then saith Jesus unto him, get thee hence, Satan: for it is written, Thou shalt worship the Lord thy God, and him only shalt thou serve."* (Matthew 4:10) *"And fear not them which kill the body, but are not able to kill the soul: but rather fear him which is able to destroy both soul and body in hell."* (Matthew 10:28)

Pray and ask God for wisdom to see through the delusions that have you in bondage. Repent of your fear and doubt. Ask God for faith and strength to face your fears. **This is the only way to break psychic control.** Pray also for the person who has been using psychic control over you, these people are usually very insecure and see control as there only way to keep relationships going. **Psychic control is broken when an individual moves from fear to faith and confidence.**

18. When the Devil Comes!!

It was just a simple exchange of words on the way home that started the argument between Rod and Sharon. But, by the time they reached home and pulled into the driveway, the disagreement had escalated. Sharon walked into the bedroom, Rod was at her heels, but before he could rest his briefcase down inside the walk-in closet, he made another remark that sent his wife of eleven years into a rage.

All of a sudden the room was aflame as words and accusations bounced from one set of lips to the other. The words were quick and sharp, cutting deep into the couple's already offended spirits. Emotional blood splattered from the deadly accusations and hurtful remarks, but the couple did not stop. Each continued, trying to get their point across and have the last word. The abuse continued and the verbal axe came down in unpleasant and insensitive statements that left deep spiritual wounds.

Unseen, a dark sinister figure rocked back and forth in the swivel bar stool in the corner of the room. He was consumed with glee. "Ha..ha ha..ha", he howled. "How I love when they fight with words like this, and this one went deeper than I expected, ha ha ha ha!" As anger consumed Sharon's heart, she began to hurl things across the room. Pulling down the tablecloth and whatever else her hand touched, she screamed at her husband, "I hate you, I hate you." Rod, too angry to speak as he watched his favorite cologne bottle hit the floor in pieces, walked out of the bedroom.

With a look of disgust toward his wife, he slammed the bedroom door behind him. Neither realized that unseen enemy was tempting and manipulating their behavior. They were totally unaware that the devil had come, and now he was about to walk away, satisfied that seeds of destruction had been deeply implanted into another marriage relationship. He knew that except this husband or wife cried out to the Lord for help, this too would be a marriage on the rocks.

> *"The thief cometh not, but for to steal, and to kill, and to destroy: I am come that they might have life, and*

that they might have it more abundantly." (John 10:10)

"Be sober, be vigilant; because your adversary the devil, as a roaring lion, walketh about, seeking whom he may devour:" (1 Peter 5:8)

"Lest Satan should get an advantage of us: for we are not ignorant of his devices." (2 Corinthians 2:11)

"<u>For God is not the author of confusion</u>, but of peace, as in all churches of the saints." (1 Corinthians 14:33)

Several years ago, the Lord revealed to me that the earth was being flooded. **"Not, of water but of spiritual death"**, he said; spiritual death where victims find themselves drowning in a sea of pride, unforgiveness, bitterness, hatred, self-righteousness and the like. The Bible states, *"This know also, that in the last days perilous times shall come.* ***For men shall be lovers of their own selves****, covetous, boasters, proud, blasphemers, disobedient to parents, unthankful, unholy, Without natural affection, trucebreakers, false accusers, incontinent, fierce, despisers of those that are good, Traitors, heady, highminded, lovers of pleasures more than lovers of God; Having a form of godliness, but denying the power thereof: from such turn away." (1 Timothy 3:1-5)*

I have no doubt that we are living in this critical time. A time of unthinkable arrogance and deceitfulness that is designed to produce *in **every living person a spirit of bitterness, unforgiveness and total selfishness as we spiritually bruise each other.*** We bruise or hurt each other because we are blinded by the pain in our own spirits. I think we have all experienced the betrayal and selfishness of our time that has injured our hearts.

When we are spiritually injured we grow callous and unforgiving, thus, we lack the sensitivity and genuine love to help or heal others. We view life and relationships from behind our padded cells of self-righteousness, and, instead of helping to heal we continue the ungodly cycle of hurting others. You see, if our spirits are bruised, **we can not form proper relationships**, and we must resort to manipulation, control and deceit to keep relationships going.

Our unforgiveness, bitterness and selfishness prevent our prayers from being answered. So, we are stuck in spiritual rut without spiritual power to overcome our most illusive and diabolical enemy: the Devil. *"Therefore I say unto you, What things soever ye desire, when ye pray, believe that ye receive them, and ye shall have them. And when ye stand praying, forgive, if ye have ought against any: that your Father also which is in heaven may forgive you your trespasses. But if ye do not forgive, neither will your Father which is in heaven forgive your trespasses." (Mark 11:24-26)*

The Devil's ultimate aim is to cause people to turn from God People who harbor unforgiveness; people who are selfish and self-centered become insecure, abusive and controlling. <u>**They are pawns in Satan's plan of destroying and hurting other people.**</u> Instead of trusting God, they always take matters into their own hands. They don't listen to advice nor do they submit to lawful authority.

However, if we understand the working of the Satan, we can recognize, resist and defeat his plans in our lives. One thing that is paramount in understanding of the Devil is he is a **dellusionist** (new English word). A dellusionist is one who makes or causes people to believe in false information. Jesus called Satan the father of lies. <u>**Satan's lies are false and misleading thoughts**</u>. The Devil controls people by feeding their minds with lies. Lies about their mate; lies about situations; lies about God; lies about life and the list goes on.

Lies are a means of making people feel insecure. Insecurity is the <u>absence of faith and trust</u>. Trust is the foundation of any relationship, and when trust is destroyed the relationship will crumble. Remember the first lie that was told: *"And the serpent said unto the woman, Ye shall not surely die: For God doth know that in the day ye eat thereof, then your eyes shall be opened, and ye shall be as gods, knowing good and evil." (Genesis 3:5)*

In tempting Eve, Satan moved from a position of insecurity to pride. First, make you doubt or disbelieve the word of God, then influence you to make a decision without God. This is his modus operandi. So when the Devil comes or begins his work on a relationship, he begins with insecurity. He wants to make you feel that the other person doesn't really love you. "Look what they have done...look how many times they have done it." He wants you to move from a position of trust and faith to an isolated position of selfish thinking and insecurity or lack of trust.

In the book of Amos, chapter three, the question is asked, *"Can two walk together except they be agreed."* **Marriage is about one; two people becoming one unit. By serving God and walking in accordance with his words toward each other strengthens the relationship.** Satan's plan, of course, is the total opposite: take care of yourself. **In other words, be married but live single.** Selfish people are controlled by their insecurities and fears, thus, their decision-making centers on themselves rather that serving the best interest of the relationship.

For most people, they can see the Devil in their husband or wife, but they forget that the Devil is an expert in delusions and trickery. One trick that the Devil uses on mankind over and over again is accusation and fault finding. This causes us to illuminate the problems in others and minimize the issues that we struggle with ourselves.

We accuse our mates of something that is wrong in their lives, then use that problem to demean and destroy them rather than help them. Then, in our deceit, we cover and trivialize our mistakes and character faults so that we can look good. We are ignorant of the fact that we are fulfilling Satan's plans of divide and conquer.

Satan attacks the character of a believer or any one who is doing good to cause insecurity. Destroying the credibility of a person's character is his way of diminishing their influence and effectiveness. And when credibility is destroyed, it becomes hard for a marriage partner to listen and receive. The relationship cannot grow and develop because trust is destroyed. Trust is the foundation of relationships.

To defeat the enemy, we must have our anchor or faith in God, not people. People will fail us. Our wives and husbands will fail us. Our children will fail us. We can not trust in them. We must put our trust in an All-powerful God. So, even when our husbands or wives fail, we can respond in faith and love to restore such a one in the spirit of meekness.

Love covers a multitude of sins, and faith is our victory. For some people, this advices sounds like ignorance. If my husband is abusive, if my wife is cheating, or if my mate have deceived and offended me, how can faith and love be the answer? The truth of the matter is that we must remember, God is the one who *allowed* it, he is the only one that can pull us through it!

Our mistake is usually doing things without God's guidance. Even though he has admonished us in his word to acknowledge him in all our ways, pride and selfishness constantly tells us that we can do things without his help. However, when we walk on without God, matters always take a turn for the worst. Our only resort is to turn back to God for his advice and wisdom.

We fuss and fight because we are in bondage to Satan plans of destroying each other through verbal abuse. Totally unaware of the demonic forces controlling and manipulating our thoughts and circumstances, we bellow out our hurts and accusations.

Only faith and love are successful against the sinister onslaught of Satan. *"For whatsoever is born of God overcometh the world: and this is the victory that overcometh the world, **even our faith**."* (1 John 4:5) Faith that God is always in control and love that can not fail. Love denies self the need to respond. Love believes in forgiveness and reconciliation. Loves opens the door for the wisdom of God to give direction and timely advice.

When I'm talking about faith and love, I'm not talking about a presumptuous person making silly decisions. For example, your husband is abusive whether verbally or physically. Some people attempt to be a doormat hoping that the person would change because of their "pseudo" love. And, instead of fleeing to a safe house or getting some type of help, they allow the abuse to go on unchecked.

This is not God's way. God is all-knowing and all-powerful and he only needs someone to obey his advice. I am reminded of a lady's husband who very abusive physically. She refused to give up on her marriage and her husband and decided to fight back! No, not physically, she fought back spiritually. She went on a fast and prayed for God to deliver her husband.

The Holy Spirit spoke to her heart and told her to anoint her home with oil (anointing oil). She did. When her husband came home, he became frantic as he entered the front door of the house. He kept saying, "there is blood every where...there is blood every where!" After a while of this, he dropped to his knees and begged God for forgiveness for abusing his wife.

This man became a Christian and never again abused his wife. I will say this to anyone whether you have a bipolar wife or husband, whether they are abusive or controlling: Go to God. The Bible says that the weapons of our warfare are powerful. *"(For the weapons of our warfare are not carnal, but mighty through God to the pulling down of strongholds;)" (2 Corinthians 10:4)*

Only God has the wisdom to defeat and destroy the works of Satan. People are destroyed because they don't have the knowledge and understanding of the working of God. *"My people are destroyed for lack of knowledge: because thou hast rejected knowledge, I will also reject thee, that thou shalt be no priest to me: seeing thou hast* forgotten the *law of thy God, I will also forget thy children." (Hosea 4:6)* We are in a spiritual fight and without properly adoring ourselves in spiritual amour and without prayer and fasting, we can not and will not overcome the works of the Devil.

Remember, your road to victory when the Devil comes will be based on two things. 1. Your knowledge of spiritual weapons: prayer, praise and fasting. 2. Arming yourself through faith, hope, love and wisdom. A good place to start is Ephesians 6, then Isaiah 58, always remembering that our problems are usually caused by our own stubborn arrogant ways. If we can simply humble ourselves before God in prayer and fasting we can get results. *"If my people, which are called by my name, shall humble themselves, and pray, and seek my face, and turn from their wicked ways; then will I hear from heaven, and will forgive their sin, and will heal their land." (2 Chronicles 7:14)*

Some time ago, I was talking to my neighbor and she gave me some good advice. She said that if you are ever caught in a fire, remember to drop and roll. She was not talking about a physical fire; she was talking about the fires of conflict. She said that most people in life get burned (emotionally/spiritually) because they neglect this one thing.

If you are in a heated conversation, humble yourself, be the one to take the low road. Be the one to offer peace or simply be quiet...drop and roll! Many of us don't realize that we are fighting a spiritual force that is more powerful than us and our only recourse is to roll into the arms of Jesus. Yes, when the Devil comes, we can have victory if we drop and roll into the arms of Jesus!

19. Divine Unity

Nothing is sweeter in a marriage than husband and wife walking in one accord. I'm not talking about a partner giving up their right to choose or becoming a "yes" person to please the other partner. I'm talking about having the same focus and outlook. Jesus prayed to the Father, *"That they all may be one; as thou, Father, art in me, and I in thee, that they also may be one in us: that the world may believe that thou hast sent me." (John 17:21)* This was his ultimate desire.

Jesus' ultimate aim was for all believers to walk in unity, having a mind and heart full of love and peace. We must remember, however, that the only way to divine unity is through a divine relationship with the Lord, he is the mediator, and the only way that there can be divine unity in a marriage.

Trying to make divine unity happen on your own is impossible. And, will lead to heartache and delusion. Only God can bring about divine unity in your marriage through brokenness and humility. In other words, both partners have to be broken (broken from pride and self-centeredness) individually by God. **<u>Again, this is strictly a God work</u>**.

This, we must accept. However, we can facilitate the work of the Holy Spirit in our marriage by humbling ourselves before him. In other words, we have to cast out and repent of stubbornness and pride. Repent of a my-way spirit. Repent of a controlling and dominating spirit.

After we have done this, we must open the door to humility and submission: Keys to divine favor and mercy. People who fuss and fight are arrogant, believing that they are right, they want to bring the other person into to line with their thinking. This is wrong and will never be right!!

Only God can change people; only he can change the heart of a husband or wife. *"The king's heart is in the hand of the LORD, as the rivers of water: he turneth it whithersoever he will." (Proverbs 21:1)* We facilitate change by being a good listener and accepting people for who they are without trying to change them.

To fuss and fight is trying to do the work of God. If you want to bring unity to your marriage, you must depend on God and His timing. Many of our arguments could be avoided if we patiently waited on the Lord; patiently waited on his direction on when to approach our spouses on a particular subject.

Or, simply keep quiet during a heated exchange for the right word, not spoken in anger, but in love. You see, humility and submission looks beyond the petty control because it's not our way, but His. Not my way Lord, I want yours! I don't need to have control over my wife or husband; I simply want to please you.

So, even though things don't go my way, I yield myself to you. Like the song-writer says, *"Perfect submission all is at rest, I and my savior are happy and bless."* When we have peace and love in our spirit, we exhibit it by offering it to our mates.

There are indeed times when in order to have peace in our marriages, we must confront issues that divide us. It could be inconsideration by a partner. It could be an injustice or something more grievous, whatever the case, our purpose is resolution and peace and not injury. When we are seeking punishment and injury to another we have become the Devil's tools and the very pit that we dig for someone to fall into, will be our trap and undoing.

Seeking reconciliation and unity is a God thing. We can not achieve it on our own; however, it should be every married partner's goal. And, when we cannot see eye to eye, we leave it to God. This is the maturity and humility that we must strive for that brings the peace that we desire. God is peace. He is the only one that can bring true peace to a relationship as we leave matters in his awesome hands.

Part Five

Victory in the Bedroom

He brought me to the banqueting house, and his banner over me was love. Stay me with flagons, comfort me with apples: for I am sick of love. His left hand is under my head, and his right hand doth embrace me. I charge you, O ye daughters of Jerusalem, by the roes, and by the hinds of the field, that ye stir not up, nor awake my love, till he please.

—Songs of Solomon 2:4-7

Introduction

*Lovemaking is one of the most wonderful
gifts given to man. Yet, very few are able to properly use this gift. In many
marriages, lovemaking is a problem area.
They simply can't get it right! On the
other hand, there are still
marriages that are
yet to explore and
appreciate the
beauty
and
pure
ecstasy of
lovemaking. Whatever
the case, I believe that part five can help you. This is not a
manual; rather it's a quick reference guide
to set you on the right track. Yes, God wants to bless
you...right in the bedroom! As you read these chapters, my
prayer is that you would be inspired to reach for the stars
and experience what lovemaking was really meant to be.*

20. The Problem

The pain was excruciating. It was the third night in a row that Eddie had gone to bed without sex. To make matters worse, Pam was about to take a trip to Tampa to visit her parents adding another eight days to his already painful ordeal. He was angry.

For Pam, it was not about the sex. They needed to settle the argument that they had the day before about spending and budgeting. And, if she couldn't get her mind into it, then lovemaking would have to wait. This had become a big part of their rollercoaster marriage; up and down, then up and down again. Their love life was never consistent, and it was taking a toll on their relationship.

Eddie was frustrated that he was being served small "kiddie" slices when he had a man-sized sexual appetite. He needed more, but how to get his wife to cooperate? It always became an argument when he brought the subject up. "Was this just the way things were to be?" he thought to himself.

Eddie got out of the bed and walked into the living room. His mind was racing. He thought about the girl at the convenience store. She had a sweet and sexy personality, and she was always nice to him....then there was Cleo at work who had a figure like a Victoria's Secret model...and not to forget Carol next door who although a little overweight, always made him feel like a giant of-a-man.

The thoughts were pounding in his mind. He needed some sexual relief and he needed it now! A noise in the kitchen startled him and brought him back to reality. It was Pam. She couldn't sleep either and was getting something from the refrigerator. Seeing Eddie on the sofa, she walked over and slumped down beside him.

The sweet smell of perfume and revealing negligee only aggravated his problem.

"Eddie, do you think we should go for counseling."

"Pam, we don't need a counselor to explain to us how and when to have sex...it's natural!"

"Well, I think we need help."

"What we need are two people willing to give their all and not some."

"Eddie, I'm willing to give my all...but it takes time. I can't just make love when so many things are troubling my mind...I want to honey...but.."

It wasn't much but it was enough to settle Eddie's irritability. "Okay....okay....let's start over." With that said, they both walked back into the bedroom and tonight....just tonight; they could have victory in the bedroom.

* * *

It is with much excitement and anticipation that couples look forward to the joys of sexual relations as a part of the marital package deal. The sexual side of a marital relationship, while being the ultimate act of pleasure, is also one of Satan's main areas to bring frustration, confusion and separation. When couples enter marriage with wrong ideas and inadequate information about their sexuality, it only adds to the already lengthy list of problems that they have to face.

Our sexually charged environment has confused men and women alike, who have allowed the media, past experiences, friends, and parents to distort their views about sex and the role it plays in marriage. However, we need not lose hope! *The pathway to pure and satisfying lovemaking can still be found. All it takes is a bit of humility and patience to find it!!*

21. Her Side

When we got married in 1985, both of us were young. Lambert had been a Christian for almost three years but previously had sexual experiences as a non-Christian. I had been a church attendant for my entire life and a Christian for almost ten years. I had no sexual experience. Having absolutely no knowledge about lovemaking in marriage except from what I overheard from friends, I didn't know what to expect. So, I bought some romantic Christian literature for both of us.

I believe it helped. We enjoyed our honeymoon! However, even now, after twenty-three years of marriage, we are still growing to understand each others needs. I believe that this is a test of our faith and a part of the Christian experience of unselfish living.

My advice to men is simple. The scripture says, *"Husbands, love your wives, even as Christ loved the church, and gave himself for it:...(Ephesians 5:25)* Remember, love suffereth long and is kind, is not puffed up....... (1 Corinthians 13:4) We need to be loved! Love in the morning with kind words and a hug; love at midday with a phone call, love in the afternoon with extra help about the house.

Love by being a good provider and spiritual protector. When a man demonstrates unselfish love, it's easier for a woman to respond to him sexually and emotionally. This does not mean that all marital problems will be cured by a loving and caring man. However, when a man demonstrates love in a tangible way, he adds leverage and weight to his masculine role.

One attribute of love that I believe is essential to a woman, especially as it relates to lovemaking, is patience. We have been created differently from our male spouses. Our emotional and psychological mindset makes us more responsive and connected to our environment: children, the bills and so on. So, it takes us more time to unwind and to get these things out of our minds.

That's why the right atmosphere and right time is crucial for a women making love or better enjoying lovemaking. Sometimes you may have to turn the lights down low. Or, the sexual prelude may have to take the form of a long stimulating conversation. Sometimes you may have start with a little romantic music. Whatever it takes to motivate and stimulate her senses, will open the door to her heart and invite your advances.

Remember, the man who is willing to look beyond his own needs and meet the needs of his wife will always be a great lover in the bedroom. The challenge will always be patience and understanding, however, your perseverance will pay-off in the end.

22. His Side

When Kim gave me a book that taught about lovemaking in marriage before we got married, I was a little embarrassed. I was confident that I would know what to do; however, after reading the book, I was glad that I got the added information.

I was able to put some of the information to use on our honeymoon, and during the early stages of our marriage; it helped me build a positive romantic relationship with Kim. However, books or booklets can never tailor-make our bedroom business. Every man and woman is different and we need to know what makes it work for our man or woman.

For me, as a man, lovemaking is always a way to take the romantic side of marriage to next level. Excitement, passion, fervency are some of the words that I would use to describe what lovemaking should always be: *Never a dull moment; never simply a routine; always a time to express deeply what mere words can not do.*

To every woman, this is what the average man wants. He wants someone with desire and passion to take it to the next level. Lovemaking should not be something that I give to my husband because he needs a release every forty-eight hours; not something that you get if you're a good husband who finished the honey-do list. No, lovemaking is for two space travelers willing to explore the universe together.

Although men may be turned on by what they see, it is always the response that takes the lovemaking to the next level. This is the desire of every man: to have a woman who is a partner and equal participant. *One who shares and even takes the lead to get to higher heights and greater depths of ecstasy and passion!!*

I believe that a lot of marriages have been robbed of the sweetness and pure ecstasy that lovemaking is intended to bring to marriage. Here, I'm not talking about perversion. No, I'm not talking about renting a "porno" movie then trying to do what you view. No!!

The sweetness and pure bliss of marriage comes from the two becoming one; united in their desire to please each other; united in their desire to improve and makes things better. *When a couple has reached this plateau, the richness and satisfaction of lovemaking takes on a more unique and complete meaning as they express love in a way that words and language simply cannot do.*

23. The Truth

A *good marriage is made up of* many ingredients and lovemaking is only one of them. Lovemaking can never take the place of the main ingredients of faithfulness, transparency, communication, forgiveness and unity or oneness.

However, lovemaking is a very important ingredient, and we would do well to know the ways and hows of using it. Indeed, this ingredient can sometimes determine whether you have a rewarding and fulfilling marriage or a recipe for failure. Without wisdom and understanding, your dream of ecstasy may become just another means of manipulation, control and sexual relief.

A poor sex life can cause major problems in a marriage, and if not properly addressed, can eventually lead to separation and even divorce. But, we need not lose hope! With the proper information and a humble spirit, we can indeed reach for the stars and achieve *victory in the bedroom!*

> *"Let the husband render unto the wife due benevolence: and likewise also the wife unto the husband. The wife hath not power of her own body, but the husband: and likewise also the husband hath not power of her own body, but the wife. Defraud ye not one the other, except it be with consent for a time, that ye may give yourselves to fasting and prayer, and come together again, that Satan tempt you not for your incontinency."* (1 Corinthians 7:3-5)

> *"Let thy fountains be dispersed abroad, and rivers of waters in the streets. Let them be only thine own, and not strangers with thee. Let thy fountain be blessed: and rejoice with the wife of thy youth. Let her be as the loving hind and pleasant roe; let her breasts satisfy thee at all times; and be thou ravished always with her love.*

And why wilt thou, my son, be ravished with a strange woman, and embrace the bosom of a strange woman" (Pro 5:16-20)

"A bundle of myrrh is my wellbeloved unto me; he shall lie all night betwixt my breasts." (Songs of Solomon." 1:13)

The above scriptures should be eye openers to both the Christian and those who may think that Christians are supposed to have a boring sex life. No, no, and a million times, no! Who made lovemaking? God. Then, if He did, shouldn't we allow the greatest teacher to be our guide in the bedroom? I assure you from my personal experience that you won't be disappointed. *"Thou wilt shew me the path of life: in thy presence is fullness of joy; at thy right hand there are pleasures for evermore." (Psalms 16:11)*

From the beginning of time, God intended lovemaking to have a rich bonding effect on the marriage relationship, as an act of pleasure and for procreation (childbearing). Lovemaking is a both a duty and a loving act. Regardless of the storms outside, when a couple comes together to physically satisfy each other, lovemaking should be as a healing balm that soothes and relaxes. In other words, even though life's daily challenges come our way, **we should endeavor to keep things going in the bedroom. It's not easy but it can be done.**

Sometimes it's hard for couples to have sex if their focus is elsewhere. It may be a hard day at the office, an unpaid bill or simply problems with family members. And, because of emotional attachments, it's harder for the female to shove these problems to the back of the mind than her male partner who is motivated and aroused by what he sees. However, this difference of mindsets of the male and female gender need not be an impediment to having a rewarding sexual life. Rather, it should enrich it as both partners meet each other's needs.

When a man and woman marry, they become one flesh. This one flesh relationship requires that they act unselfishly, *always considering the needs of the other person.* So, the golden rule in the bedroom should always be: **Aim to Please**. For the inexperienced male lover, this may take time to learn. However, with patience, he can learn to effectively stimulate his wife while delaying his own ejaculation until his wife has achieved an orgasm.

Likewise, the woman should aim to please her husband and never use sex as a weapon to control and manipulate her husband. This creates insecurities when the husband realizes that he is working for pay and not enjoying the freedom of making "sweet love." Contrary to old myths about a woman's sexuality, there is absolutely nothing wrong with a woman being the sexual initiator.

Many who read the Songs of Solomon miss the fact that the Shulamite woman in most instances is the initiator of the lovemaking activity. She is the one that wakes up in the night to look for midnight passion and sexual fulfillment (Songs of Solomon 3:1-5). She is the one who alludes to her lover being a bundle of myrrh who will lie all night "betwixt my breast" One night when her lover came for satisfaction, she was tired and had already gone to bed but at the sound of his voice, she arose and went looking for her lover. She was determined to be there for him. This should be a valuable lesson to today's working women (Songs of Solomon 5:2-8). One's commitment to the marriage should never take second place to work.

Technique & Communication

Poor technique can also be reasons for sexual problems. Being uninformed about sexual techniques is usually the result of the lack of understanding of the female and male physiology. Men and women who do not understand how to "turn on" their partners, even though they may be well-intentioned, can stifle fulfillment in the bedroom. *(I recommend that you purchase a book about sexual fulfillment from your local Christian bookshop, there are many Christian authors who teach on this subject. I recommend "The Act of Marriage" by Tim and Beverly Lahaye)*

Foreplay or petting should usually begin sexual fulfillment in the bedroom. The sexual organs should be gently caressed and massaged.

The best way to proceed is to touch, feel and experiment asking the other partner, at intervals, if the touch or caressing brings pleasure. Always be sensitive and remember those areas that bring the greatest pleasure. Additionally, always take care to tell your spouse how beautiful, lovely, or how strong and nicely built their body is. During the time of lovemaking, words ascribing beauty to the female and strength to male body will pay dividends in the end. Conversely, one should refrain from all and any negative remarks about their mate's body.

Proper communication is another key to eliminating problems in the bedroom. Never feel bashful to talk about the problems that you face in the bedroom. Picking the right time, and when your spouse is in the right mood may be a challenge, however, communication is your only recourse if things are going wrong. Use tact and the gentle approach to bring across your point. Everyone makes mistakes. And we are all learning daily. With that in mind, approach the matter with a humble attitude.

Finally, it is important, when possible, to dress for lovemaking. Excitement can be intensified and the mood ratcheted up if the right attire, fragrance and atmosphere are a part of the lovemaking picture. But and when the rage of passion takes over before these pleasantries can be put in place, it's always okay; the moment of passion should get first attention.

However, smelly underwear, hole-um-joe panties, faded t-shirts, bad breath, and foul body odors as a result of lack of bodily hygiene should always be avoided as these can be a turn-off. Sometimes, we forget that lovemaking doesn't end with the honeymoon. It's a lifelong thing. Try to look sexy…if that's what you are going to do.

24. Deeper Problems

There are some problems in the marriage bed that cannot be changed or remedied by simple changes in hygiene or attitude. These problems require wisdom, prayer and deliverance. In most cases, these problems are a carry over from previous sexual experiences that were never dealt with by forgiveness or repentance. As a result, these problems raise their stubborn heads in the marriage bed refusing to budge.

For example, the young promiscuous girl who doesn't realize that her frequent sexual encounters will cause emotional damage with hurt feelings, bipolar problems, and then, physically in the destruction of her vaginal muscles. Similarly, the young man who believes that every young woman is a "score" gets a herpes infection, that he eventually carries into his marriage. Or worse, he never learns to discipline his sexual desires, and struggles with infidelity.

These youthful mistakes at the time seem trivial, however, for the young woman, the vagina may never be snug without a surgical operation. And only forgiveness for oneself and true repentance toward God, can cure and heal the deeper spiritual and psychological wounds. For the young man, the same is also true, medical treatment, and likewise forgiveness and repentance.

Sexual Addiction

There are a number of reasons why a person may be suffering from sexual addition. If you believe that your husband or wife may have an abnormal sexual appetite (abnormal doesn't mean that the person may desire sex more than you do, abnormal means that the person has no control or discipline) then use extreme wisdom, tact and much prayers. Although your spouse may be suffering from bondage in this area, to insult or scorn the offender only deepens the problem. This can create resentment and can result in further marital problems. Use love. Love never fails.

When people open their lives up to pornography of any kind, they open themselves up to demonic spirits. I remember a lady telling my wife and me, how she had rented some videos from the local Blockbuster store to spruce up lovemaking in her marriage. She said that after viewing the videos she developed an insatiable appetite for sex. Eventually, it became a problem in her marriage because her husband couldn't keep up with the well-oiled freight train.

She said that it wasn't until she quit watching pornography and with much prayer that her sexual drive became normal again. Remember, if you open the door to pornography, it's very hard to close. Sex then becomes an animalistic act of selfish pleasure rather than mutual pleasure; fulfilling a fantasy becomes the most important thing. This causes problems both spiritually and physically for the other partner who can't keep up.

In the same vein, a person who had been sexually active before marriage, may still have a sexual spirit present in their lives and only the power of God's spirit can displace it. These are the people who appear sexually competent before marriage but become sexually unfilled in their own marriages because expectations are not met. Or desire may wane because sexual intercourse alone cannot keep them faithful. As a result, they may seek sexual fulfillment outside the marriage bond.

In the same vein, sexual intercourse is a God-given gift meant to nurture the marriage relationship. If your husband or wife wants to participate in sexual activity that is unnatural or offensive to you, you have a right to confront them. Let your spouse know and state your reasons, but remember sometimes our sexual preferences have been molded by our upbringing or experiences. This means that what one partner may deem repulsive may not be to the other. Sexual acts should be agreed upon before you reach the bedroom; a partner should not perform a sexual act that may offend the other partner. *"Let us therefore follow after the things which make for peace, and things wherewith one may edify another. For meat destroy not the work of God. All things indeed are pure, but it is evil for that man who eateth with offense. It is good neither to eat flesh, nor to drink wine, nor any thing whereby thy brother stumbleth, or is offended, or is made weak. Hast thou faith? Have it to thyself before God. Happy is he that condemneth not himself in that thing which he alloweth. And he that doubteth is damned if he eat because he eateth not of faith, for whatsoever is not of faith is sin." (Romans 14:19-23)*

In addition, and now that I'm a bit older, some sexual acts now being performed by marital partners have been borrowed from homosexuals, and if performed in the marriage bed, can open up the door for perverted sexual spirits to enter the marriage. Anal sex is just one of them. When you have crossed this line, sexual fulfillment is no longer possible as we seek more and more avenues to increase intensity by purely physical means not realizing that we are no longer in control, but are now the slaves of our demonic hosts.

If this is your case, repent! Seek God's forgiveness and that of your partner. Cleanse your life through renouncing and turning from these perverted acts. Remember, your desire for intense and satisfying sex can only come from a genuine and loving relationship.

Lack of Performance

Frigidity, mostly found among women, is when a partner has difficulty performing sexually or may not be able to function at all. This can be caused by a number of reasons which include traumatic past sexual experiences like rape or incest. In this case, it may be beneficial to enlist the services of a trained counselor or pastor who is well-versed in this field. However, if the frigidity is caused by spurious information regarding sex, passed on to the married partner i.e. sexual intercourse is evil or dirty. Then patience, prayer, coaching and teaching (scriptures that show that God encourages a vibrant sex life) may be the easy solution. However, if the problem persists counseling may be the only recourse.

I remember a young lady who had been a member of our denomination who would get dressed in the closet or in the dark and always made love under the covers. Even after many years of marriage, she found it difficult to undress in the front of her husband. This became a problem in the marriage that required Pastoral counseling. I believe that it was eventually resolved and the young lady found healing and deliverance.

This is an example of frigidness. Whatever the reason, the young lady couldn't function sexually in the marriage. There could have been a past traumatic incident in her life or it could be a religious spirit that was hindering her from having a normal sexual relationship with her husband.

25. Keeping Romantic Love Alive

Adjacent to the mental and spiritual problems, couples may experience a waning in sexual activity if they do not keep themselves healthy and fit by exercising regularly, eating and supplementing their diet with essential vitamins. A lot of men and women, after a few years of marriage or as they grow older, minimize the need to stay fit.

I realize that with age and after children the weight comes and the metabolism slows down. However, we can still keep our lovemaking fresh and our vitality into our twilight years if we simply take care of our bodies through diet and exercise. Just the other day, my wife told me that I needed to do something with my stomach because it was getting in the way (you know). So, I'm doing those crunches every day. We can do it!!

Additionally, couples who suffer from chronic ailments like diabetes that reduce potency should seek the assistance of a qualified physician for advice and information that can improve their lovemaking. Although there are potency drugs on the market like Viagra, one's physician should always be consulted before taking these pharmaceuticals. One's doctor should also be consulted regarding exercise, diet, and vitamins to ensure that it is safe and conforms to the needs of each partner.

Keep the Fire Burning

<u>Desire is the catalyst for passion</u>. The desire to be together or closeness ignites passion. Passion dies when this desire or interest is elsewhere. It may be the new job, a baby, or the daily frustrations of life. Whatever is keeping you from pleasing your mate will no doubt put water on the fire of passion. **Refocus**. Remember why you got married. Remember, how it was the first time you met. Remember how you couldn't keep your hands of each other. If you have passion, you can keep it, or you can always get it back, if you put first things first. **Aim to please.**

Without passion, our marriages become mechanical and lifeless. We choose when and when not to make love. Lovemaking becomes an intrusion into our daily affairs and more duty or stress reliever rather than a loving act. But, this need not be the case. When passion wanes in my marriage, I pray. I ask God to restore what the enemy has come to destroy. Then, I cooperate with the Holy Spirit as he initiates me to please my wife. You can too!

You see, to produce love in the bedroom goes far beyond proper technique, diet and exercise. To produce excellent love in the bedroom comes from a good and well-rounded relationship that is built on faith, commitment, trust, obedience, and respect. Husbands and wives who fail in these main components will fail to *make love*. Love should never begin late at night, rather, it should be the order of the day. Kind words, hugs, kisses, the daily, "I love you," the listening ear, the walk in the park, time spent together just talking and sharing, should be staples of all marriages.

Finally, we must always take care that lovemaking never be the foundation that a marriage is built upon because there will be times when sexual enjoyment must be deferred because of circumstances i.e. sickness, fasting, a necessary long trip, death of a relative and such. Nonetheless, God has ordained that sex be a fulfilling and enjoyable part of the marriage relationship; and when we do it right...*it becomes a piece of heaven on earth!*

About Marriage Mechanics

Marriage Mechanics started in 1996 by husband and wife team Lambert and Kim Sands. Suffering from a recent tragedy and death of their fourth child, the couple received a divine call to marriage ministry. They started a local magazine formatted TV program called Marriage Mechanics. The program became the most popular TV program on a secular station; thus began Marriage Mechanics Ministries, a multi-facet ministry using TV, radio, and the print media to build, revitalize, and bring encouragement to couples and those contemplating marriage with a Bible-based marriage message. The Ministry relocated to the Florida area in 1998.

Lambert Sands, President of Marriage Mechanics, and originally from the Bahamas, is an ordained minister and has been in ministry for over thirty years. He is a gifted speaker and author of numerous books. He currently lives in Deltona, Florida with his two daughters after the passing of his wife in 2012.

Phone: 407 385 8201
Email: marriagemechanics@hotmail.com
Website: marriagemechanics.org

OTHER BOOKS AVAILABLE:

The Power of Submission'
Walking in Male Authority
Living Single
The Price of Dominion
Why Cancer Doesn't Scare Me Anymore!
The Treasure Box (Devotional)
The Noah Chronicles
Overcoming Jezebel, Delilah & Anger

www.ingramcontent.com/pod-product-compliance
Lightning Source LLC
Chambersburg PA
CBHW031419290426
44110CB00011B/446